USING EVIDENCE

C K Macdonald

GENERAL EDITOR Jon Nichol

> **❝**The poetry of History lies in the miraculous fact that once upon this earth, on this familiar spot of ground, walked other men and women, as actual as we are today, thinking their own thoughts, swayed by their own passions, but now all gone, one generation vanishing after another, gone, as utterly as we ourselves will shortly be gone, like ghosts at cock-crow.**❞**
>
> G M Trevelyan (British historian)

Basil Blackwell

Contents

Introduction: History and Historians

The old man picked up his pen and tried to remember. It was hard to recall what life had been like when he was a boy. It was such a very long time ago. Everything was so different then and so much had happened since. Yet he wanted to write it all down so that future generations would know just what things were like in those days. Slowly the memories came back:

❛I was born on 26 March 1884. When I was still very small there was an old woman who was a widow living in a run down little house near us. She seemed close to starvation. One day she came out of her garden gate and collapsed. I saw her taken away in a horse-drawn van. She died a day or two later in Petworth Workhouse, probably from starvation. Old people often had very little to live on and so they relied a good deal on charity. Sometimes old people without children were forced to leave their homes and go into the workhouse. These were dreaded places. A poor husband and wife would be separated at the workhouse door and unless someone offered help they would never live together again . . .❜ (A)

Do you ever spread rumours? Have you noticed how rumours often change and the details of what really happened are forgotten? Suppose the old man had not written down his memories but simply *told* his story to his children. They might forget some of the details, get their facts wrong, or exaggerate what had happened. Slowly the story would change. It would become more and more difficult to know which parts were true. **B** is from a Viking *saga* (legend). It describes events that may have taken place about 1000 years earlier. The events were first written down several hundred years after they are supposed to have taken place:

❛Skarphedin and the other four warriors set off in search of an enemy called Thrain. They found him but he was on the other side of an icy river and had seven men with him. They charged down to the river's edge . . . Skarphedin took a running start and leapt forward on to the icefloe, where Thrain was, with the speed of a bird. Thrain was just about to put on his helmet as Skarphedin bore down on him and struck him with his axe "Battle Troll". The axe split Thrain's head right down so that his teeth dropped onto the ice. This happened so quickly that no one could strike at Skarphedin and he continued to glide along the ice at great speed.❜ (B)

Do you think this is a true story? Which bits do you suspect may be untrue?

A and **B** are both evidence about the past. They are clues about things that happened long ago. As historians,

D Aerial photographs sometimes show up archaeological evidence which cannot be seen from the ground

we use evidence to try to piece together what people did in the past and how they did it. Look around you. You are surrounded by history. All round your home town, village, or city there is evidence about its past. Houses, schools, churches, pubs, roads, paths, ruins, place names, street names and the landscape are all silently reminding us that other people have walked the Earth before us. The historian A L Rowse points out:

❛. . . beneath the towns and villages, the roads and fields of today we may construct under our very eyes, out of the pieces of evidence that remain, a picture of another age.❜ (C)

Many clues lie buried beneath the ground, like **D**. Pages 8–11 look at how **archaeologists** use such evidence to piece together the past. Sometimes all physical remains have gone. **E** is another aerial photograph. It shows an ancient settlement in Oxfordshire. Nothing

E The remains of an ancient settlement in Oxfordshire

can be seen of the site from the ground. It was only discovered when this photograph was taken. **Photographs** have many different uses for historians, as pages 13–15 show. The historian A L Rowse continues:

There are other types of evidence that tell us something of what we long to know. Sources which tell us more but are no less incomplete and with mysterious silences. These are written documents. **(F)**

A and **B** are two such **written documents**. **A** is a fairly easy source for historians to use: it was written for just that purpose. But most documents are not written with historians in mind, they are simply to do with people's daily lives. A L Rowse tells us:

There are the letters that dead men and women have written to each other about their business affairs, or about their private views, their feelings for their friends, their families and their griefs. Then sometimes there are diaries, a rare source indeed. **(G)**

Letters and **diaries** can help us to look at the lives of people who lived and died long ago. Pages 16–17 look at letters and pages 18–19 examine diaries.

Pictures and **cartoons** are also very important to historians. A few pictures are drawn with the aim of showing people in the future what things were like. **H** is a picture of King Henry VIII. It was painted so that generations to come might know just what he looked like. Pages 20–21 look at pictures and cartoons as evidence.

What's in the news today? Today's **newspapers** and TV news programmes will be important sources for future historians as they try to find out what life was like in Britain in the 1980s and 90s. But newspapers can be very misleading. Pages 22–25 look at some of the problems they pose for historians. **Biographies** are another way to find out about the powerful and the famous, the kinds of people who are often in the news. Biographies are examined on pages 26–27.

When did you last have to fill in a form for something? Believe it or not, that form might help a historian one day. All sorts of reports, registers, forms, statistics and other documents are kept by governments, businesses, churches and other bodies. Many of them end up in County Records Offices. Pages 28–29 and 30–33 show how you can examine **government documents** and **local records** to discover new facts about the past. Most of these records have never been studied by historians.

H King Henry VIII, painted by Holbein

It is *facts* that interest us as historians. The historian G M Trevelyan wrote:

In the realm of history the moment we have reason to think that we are being given fiction instead of fact, even if the fiction is ever so clever, our interest collapses like a pricked balloon. To hold our interest you must tell us something we believe to be true about the people who once walked the earth. It is the fact about the past that is important. Just because it really happened it gathers round it all the mystery of life and death and time. (J)

It may seem strange to include a chapter on **fiction** as evidence. However, as pages 34–35 show, although fiction is of little use in giving us the facts, *some* fiction can help us to *imagine* the past, and to picture what living in a certain time and place must have been like.

Do you have a good imagination? The historian J Huizinga tells us:

History is concerned with relations between people and their thoughts. The historian tries to re-live what was once experienced by people like ourselves. The true study of history involves our imagination and conjures up pictures and visions. (K)

If we are to understand what happened in the past we need to put ourselves in the position of people of the past – to try to re-live the past in our minds. Pages 36–39 show how this can be done.

In many ways historians work like detectives, trying to solve a case by piecing together the clues that people have left behind them. Pages 40–45 are a case study in which you can use many of the types of evidence examined in this book to try to solve a great historical mystery, the mystery of the *Lusitania*.

The historian Christopher Hill has written:

We are what history has made us and history will continue to have power over us whether we recognise it or not. We are what we are and our society is what it is because of hundreds of years of past struggles – for religious freedom, for juries, for the vote for men and women, against child labour (in factories and mines – see pages 28–29), *for shorter working hours, for trades unions, against censorship and for peace. We shan't all reach the same conclusions. But it will give us a better chance of understanding the present.* (L)

In some countries the government does not want people to understand the present. It does not want them to know what is going on. So it tries to control what is learned in history lessons. Pages 46–48 look at how people sometimes try to *distort* (make false) history to gain support for their own political point of view.

Using Evidence encourages you to ask questions about things, rather than just accepting things as they are without thinking about them. Studying the evidence can help us think things out for ourselves.

Using Evidence will *not* involve you in lots of writing. Many of the activities are 'open-ended'. This means your teacher, you and the rest of your class can adapt them to suit your own interests and circumstances. They aim to help you enjoy your history and to make you want to find out more. G M Trevelyan points out:

The thing which leads the historian on is his/her curiosity to know what really happened long ago in that land of mystery we call the past. History is like peering into a magic mirror and seeing fresh faces there every day.

The dead were – and are not. Their place knows them no more and is ours today. Yet they were once as real as we, and we shall tomorrow be shadows like them. (M)

The light we can throw on the past will help to show the way for the future. It is this that makes history not simply the most interesting, but also the most important subject studied in schools.

??????????????

1 The rumours game Your teacher takes one of the class outside and tells him/her a short story. That person then passes the story on to someone else and so on round the class. The last person tells what they have heard to the whole of the class. Your teacher then re-tells the original story.

   a In what ways has it changed? Why?

   b What does this tell us about evidence that has been passed on by word of mouth for many years before being written down?

2 a What does **D** show? Draw a rough plan of the site. Mark on it what you think the different shapes might be. What reasons can you think of to explain why people stopped living here?

   b What might the circles in **E** have been? They can best be seen (from the air) when there are crops growing in the field. Try and find out why this is.

3 150 years ago most people in Britain could not read or write. How does this limit the use of letters and diaries in finding out about the people of the past?

4 What impression do you get of Henry VIII from **H**? Is this the kind of impression he would want you to get? How far can we trust the painting as evidence about Henry?

5 Explain in your own words what G M Trevelyan meant in **M**.

1 Primary and Secondary Sources

The San Carlos Landings

On 21 May 1982 over 1000 British troops went ashore at Port San Carlos in the Falkland Islands. It was the biggest seaborne invasion since D-Day (the Allied invasion of Normandy in the Second World War). Patrick Bishop saw what happened:

❝*Dawn on Friday over San Carlos revealed a spectacular sight. The bay crowded with frigates* (a type of ship) *and assault ships and the air was filled with helicopters ferrying ammunition and artillery ashore. From the "Canberra" we could see troops moving over the brown peaty hills a few hundred yards away under the pale blue clear sky. The fleet had moved in close to the land to shelter from air attacks from the deadly air-launched Exocet missiles. The attack began at 5 am (British time) on Friday . . . (the) target was the San Carlos Settlement, several farms with a population of 32 men, women and children.*

. . . at 5.45 there were two small explosions over Fanning Head and lights began to flicker on the hillside. Moments later the night was shattered by the thump of gun fire from a frigate raining shells down on the surrounding area. This was the first sign that the operation would not go as smoothly as planners had hoped . . . we could see the outline of the landing craft clustering around the assault ships to collect their load, drifting away then creeping towards the shore. A destroyer and a frigate continued to pour fire at Fanning Head and at an Argentine airfield 20 miles to the south. The operation took place in the worst possible weather conditions. Planners had hoped for low cloud to hide the assault force. ❞ **(A)**

F This photograph appeared on the front pages of many British newspapers

G The San Carlos landings, as seen by a cartoonist in *The Sun*

B is by an Argentine soldier:

❝*I saw the ships arriving in the bay from the hillside where I was on patrol. The next thing I knew I was surrounded by British troops. I could not fire because I had lost my rifle. Anyway it was all too quick. An officer spoke to us in English. I think he asked us to stop and surrender. I drew my pistol and some one shot me in the leg. I had to stop.* ❞ **(B)**

A and **B** are first-hand accounts. They are by people who were there and witnessed what happened. Not all historical evidence is first-hand. Second-hand sources are also very important. **C** is a statement by John Nott, the British Minister of Defence, about the landings:

❝*These landings were not opposed and a secure land base is being set up. During the night several landings and raids were made by our forces in different parts of the islands. Some of these forces have remained ashore. The Argentines suffered losses and some prisoners have been taken. These operations continue. As we expected our ships have come under heavy air attack. Five have been damaged, two seriously. There have been some British casualties but we have no details yet. Our Harriers* (fighter planes) *have shot down and destroyed seven Mirages, five Skyhawks and two Pucaras* (planes used by the Argentines). *Seven weeks after the Argentine invasion British forces are tonight firmly established on the Falkland Islands.* ❞ **(C)**

John Nott's account is second-hand. It was based on messages he had received from the British 'Task Force'.

Clearly it is important for historians to know whether the evidence they are dealing with comes from an eye-witness or not. However, sources do not always fall neatly into one type or the other. This is shown in **D** as Patrick Bishop continues his account:

‘As the first red alert sounded aboard "Canberra" troops rushed to man the anti-aircraft guns and Blowpipe missile positions. A Pucara suddenly appeared over the hill. A stream of fire flickered from under its wing and a salvo of rockets punched into the water behind a frigate . . . After that the air attacks came thick and fast. Next to strike were two Mirages firing rockets. A Seawolf missile soared up from a frigate towards one of the escaping planes which crashed in an effort to dodge it and exploded in a ball of orange fire . . .

A few minutes after 4 am on Friday morning the manager of a lonely sheep farm was wakened by his son complaining of noises at the end of the garden. A few moments later Mr Shore answered a knock at the front door to meet an officer of the Royal Marines. By first light the troops were all strongly dug in and all round air defence was being set up.’ (D)

In **D** Patrick Bishop is describing some events which he has seen or heard himself and some which he has heard about from other people. So parts of **D** are first-hand evidence and parts second-hand.

Sources **A–D** were all produced during the Falklands War. They are *contemporary* sources (they come from the time of the event). Historians call such contemporary sources **primary** evidence and use them to piece to-gether what happened.

E is from a history of the Falklands War:

‘On 21 May Mr Nott announced that following earlier raids British forces had set up a firm bridgehead in the Falklands. Royal Marines and the Parachute Regiment went ashore in large numbers with artillery, air defence weapons and other heavy equipment. Argentine forces suffered losses and some prisoners were taken. British ships came under heavy air attack and five were damaged, two seriously. On 22 May the Task Force commander received orders from Downing Street to re-take all the islands. According to the Ministry of Defence there were now some 5000 British troops on the Falklands and they were in control of a ten square mile bridgehead.’ (E)

E and other accounts by historians are called **secondary** sources. Secondary sources are accounts or other evidence produced by historians, reporters, playwrights, TV producers and other people after examining and weighing-up the information from primary sources.

Patrick Bishop is a journalist. His account (**A** and **D**) was written for the *Observer* newspaper. **F** and **G** show how other British newspapers reported the war.

In May 1982 John Nott told the House of Commons:

‘The reports coming from the journalists in the Falkland Islands have generally speaking been magnificent. They have been clear and have given the country much information which has been of great value to us. I have nothing but praise for what the journalists there have done. All the journalists' reports are looked at down there . . . Of course we are careful to make sure that no information is released by them that would damage our forces.’ (H)

J shows the front cover of *The Listener* in May 1982.

VIEWER LISTENER GUIDE Pages 31-38

THE LISTENER

6 May 1982 Price 50p (IR 76p, USA and Canada $1.50)

The first casualty of war

Christopher Wain
Ian McDougall

tru+h

J Cover of *The Listener* magazine, 6 May 1982

??????????????

1 a How can we tell that Patrick Bishop wrote **A** and **D** soon after the San Carlos landings? How far can we trust his report?

b What point does John Nott make in **H**?

c What message is **J** trying to put across?

d What point is the photographer making in **F**?

2 What does **G** tell us about the way *The Sun* reported the Falklands War. Is it primary or secondary evidence about the San Carlos landings?

3 a Where has John Nott got his information from in **C**? In what ways has he acted like a historian?

b Where has the historian who wrote **E** got his information from?

4 What is the difference between a primary and a secondary source? In what ways might this division of evidence be misleading?

5 List other types of evidence historians might use to find out about the Falklands War. In each case, say whether the evidence is primary or secondary.

2 Archaeology and Archaeologists

What is archaeology? David Miles is an archaeologist. He tells us:

'*Archaeology is concerned with the systematic* (logical) *study of the physical remains of human communities — the surviving* structures (ruins), *pottery, tools and general debris* (bits and pieces) *that people in the past have left behind them. It differs from History in the narrow sense in that it does not rely on written evidence.*' (A)

What 'bits and pieces' will *you* leave behind you? Many of the things that you throw away might one day be of use to archaeologists. When you get home make a list of the things in your dustbin. What might other people learn about *you* and *your* way of life from the things you've thrown away?

Suppose that in one minute's time your school is destroyed in a disaster — a freak earthquake, perhaps. There are no survivors. Two thousand years go by and the disaster is long forgotten. Then workmen on a building site come across some old bones. Digging down they find ruins — the remains of your classroom. A team of archaeologists is called in. They try to find out:

- How old are these remains?
- What were these buildings?
- How old were these people when they died?
- How did they die?
- What can we learn about them and their way of life?

They try to piece together the answers to these questions from the clues you have left behind. But what would be left behind? Which things would decay and disappear completely? All wood, paper, leather, wool and cotton things would be long since gone. Things made of plastic, pottery, glass, stone or metal might well survive. Of your bodies, only the bones would probably remain (unless there is a lot of acid in the soil, in which case these too would disappear). Make a list of the things that archaeologists might find. Which of their questions might they be able to answer?

Archaeologists use many different methods to piece together the clues of long ago. They face many problems in doing so. Some of these can be seen by looking at the excavation of *Danebury*, an ancient hillfort in Hampshire, (B).

Danebury

Danebury is one of many hillforts in southern Britain believed to have been built during the Iron Age (from about 600 BC to the beginning of the Roman Conquest

B Danebury from the air

of Britain in AD 43). At this time people living in Britain were mainly 'Celts'. Celts also lived in France and Ireland. In 1968 Barry Cunliffe and a team of archaeologists began to study the Danebury area. They wanted to know the answers to the questions in C (and many more).

Danebury is a *prehistoric* site. Prehistory refers to all of human past (about two million years) up to the time when men and women started to write things down. In Britain things were not written down (as far as we know) until the first Roman invasion in 55 BC. So Barry Cunliffe could not look at written sources left by people who lived at Danebury — because there aren't any!

People often think that to find out about a site archaeologists simply *excavate* it (dig into it). In fact, they only excavate a site as a last resort. They always look for other clues first. These may include:

C Questions Barry Cunliffe and his team asked

- Was Danebury really a hillfort?
- Was there ever a village or town there – or was it just a refuge during wartime?
- If it *was* a hillfort, was it ever attacked?
- When was it built?
- How many people lived there?
- When did people stop living there?
- What were their homes like?
- How did they make their living – were they mainly hunters or farmers? If farmers, what kind of farming?
- Did people travel much or did most people stay in one area all their lives?
- What were their religious beliefs, if any?
- How important was Danebury and the people who lived there?

Old maps and place-names Old maps show that 'Danebury' is a fairly new name (it used to be called 'Dunbury'). Like most place-names in the south of England it is not a Celtic name but Saxon. Most of the old Celtic names are long forgotten.

Aerial photographs Photographs taken from the air often show up ancient sites even if they cannot be seen from the ground. Aerial photographs show that Danebury was once surrounded by ancient farmhouses.

Archaeological records It is important to check these, to make sure that other archaeologists have not already found out what you want to know.

Fieldwork Cunliffe's team carried out a careful survey of the Danebury area.

Excavation In August 1969 Cunliffe's team began to excavate Danebury. The work is still going on.

Another archaeologist tells us:

❝*Excavations can be exciting. They get in the news and they appeal to the imagination. They are also expensive, hard work, and in a sense destructive.' When archaeologists excavate a site they take it to pieces.* ❞ (**D**)

This is one reason why archaeologists always record what they find and precisely where they find it. At Danebury all the information was fed into a computer.

F Methods of dating archaeological finds

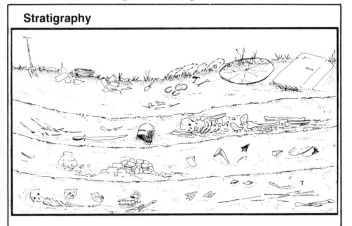

Stratigraphy

Carbon-14 dating
All living things contain carbon-14. When a creature dies the carbon-14 begins to decay. By measuring the amount of carbon-14 left in *organic* remains (remains that were once living, such as wood or bone) archaeologists can work out roughly how old they are. Many of the organic materials found at Danebury could be dated to about the nearest 70 years. Carbon-14 dating is of little use for remains that are over 60 000 years old.

Potassium–Argon dating
Many objects contain potassium. Potassium-40 slowly decays to argon-40. By measuring the amount of argon-40 in the potassium archaeologists can work out the age of the object.

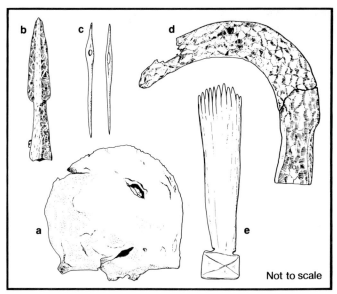

Not to scale

G These objects were found at Danebury. What do you think they are?

Cunliffe says the aim of this was:

❝*to record everything in enough detail to be able to reconstruct on paper and in words what the excavation destroyed.* ❞ (**E**)

Knowing in what *layer* of the ground something was found can help archaeologists to date an object. Usually, the deeper the layer is, the older the object will be. This method of dating is called *stratigraphy* ('strata' means layers). **F** shows how it works. Archaeologists use many other methods of dating. Two of the most important are *carbon-14* dating and *potassium-argon* dating (see **F**).

Cunliffe's team have to identify the things they find. **G** shows a few of the things found at Danebury.

?????????????

1 What does 'prehistory' mean? Why do we know so little about it?

2 Why do archaeologists only excavate as a last resort' (**D**)?

3 a What are the objects shown in **G**?
b What do they tell us about the community at Danebury?

4 a What three methods do archaeologists use to date finds (see **F**)?
b Can you think of any other ways they might be able to date things? (Emptying your pockets may help you here.)

5 Look at **G**. Object **a** is in fact the forehead of a human skull. What is there to suggest that this person died violently? One of the other objects can help you work out how he/she died.

3 Danebury – Making Sense

Table **A** gives a few of the findings from the excavations at Danebury. Read them carefully, then look back at **C** on page 8 – the questions Barry Cunliffe's team of archaeologists asked when they began to study Danebury.

The findings in **A** tell us a lot about the Iron Age people who lived at Danebury. They partly answer some of our questions. But they also raise many new points (**D**).

You may be able to think of other questions you want to know the answers to.

A What archaeologists discovered at Danebury

Ramparts Stratigraphy and carbon dating suggests that the huge ramparts (see **B** and **G**) were built between 600 and 500 BC. The ramparts were rebuilt and strengthened at least three times. The main east entrance had an outer gate and an inner gate. It was cleverly designed so that if an attacking army tried to break through the inner gate it could be shot at from all sides.

Main gates About 100 BC the main gates were burnt down. There are no traces of any new gates since then.

Remains of tools – on the floors of some of the excavated buildings. Stratigraphy suggests they had been there since about 100 BC. Few of the artefacts discovered are less than 2100 years old.

Human remains – of about 100 bodies (**C**). Some show terrible injuries (such as the skull in **G** on page 9). Often human skulls have been found lying by themselves. Carbon-14 dating shows that these people died at various times from about 550–100 BC. The last pit to have been dug at Danebury contained the bodies of 21 people, males and females between the ages of 4 and 45. The pit appeared to have been left uncovered and then silted up.

Stones – thousands of small, smooth, round stones. One pit near the east gate contained 11 000. Some were found on the ramparts and many were found in the east entrance area.

Weapons – many spear heads and javelin heads have been found but no swords.

Holes Barry Cunliffe reports: *'The surface of the hill is peppered with holes of all sizes. In all we estimate there were about 5000 storage pits dug in Danebury and about 18 000 post holes.'* The post holes held the foundations of wooden buildings, most of which were round. At any one time there seem to have been about 50–60 buildings. Cunliffe says: 'In the latest phase (of the fort) the resident population (numbers living there) could have been about 200–350.

Animal bones – 14 000, mostly sheep, goats and cattle. The remains of dogs, horses and ravens were found buried by themselves at the bottom of some pits. Ravens do not naturally live in the area in large numbers.

Seeds – burnt remains mainly of wheat and barley (carbon dated to between 600 and 100 BC).

Farming tools – including metal tips of several *ards* (a simple kind of plough).

Pottery – over 100 000 *sherds* (pieces of pottery), the remains of vases, saucepans, and jars. Later ones were made of brickearth, which is not found locally.

Weaving combs, loom weights and needles.

Iron bars.

Parts of iron furnaces.

B The main ramparts and eastern gate of the Danebury hillfort

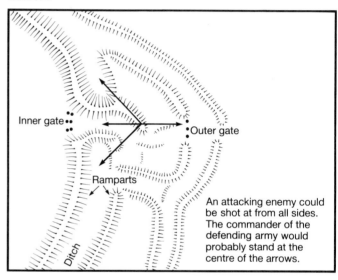

Inner gate · · Outer gate
Ramparts
Ditch

An attacking enemy could be shot at from all sides. The commander of the defending army would probably stand at the centre of the arrows.

C Some of the human remains found at Danebury

D More questions about Danebury

- What was stored in the big pits? Could it have been grain? Wouldn't grain rot if it was stored underground?
- Had the ramparts and the main gates been burned in an attack? Why might someone have wanted to attack Danebury?
- Why were there so many small round stones on the ramparts and at the main entrance?
- Why were no swords found at Danebury?
- Why did many of the human remains at Danebury show signs of terrible injuries?
- What happened to the remains of the thousands of other people who lived at Danebury over the centuries?
- Why were human skulls found lying by themselves?
- Why were ravens, dogs and horses found at the bottom of many pits?

Archaeologists have managed to piece together possible answers to some of these points by looking at other clues. They have carried out experiments which help to explain some of their finds. They know that there were other Celtic tribes living in Ireland and France. Written records about some of these have survived, which can give archaeologists clues about the Celts at Danebury. (Of course, Celtic tribes in France and Ireland may have been very different from those in southern Britain.) Studying simple farming societies that still exist today may also tell us something about the people of Iron Age Danebury.

G

Table **E** gives some of these other sources of information. Study them carefully. Then try to answer the points in **D**.

Most of these kinds of questions can never be answered for certain. There are no 'correct' answers. As we have seen, archaeologists, like all historians, have to work out the most likely explanation. We have to make estimates, we have to guess, we have to use our imaginations. As Barry Cunliffe points out:

Standing on a bare hilltop in the pouring rain watching the mud wash down over a freshly excavated chalk floor reminds one of the enormous gap between life as it was led and the sparseness (small amount) of the archaeological record. (**F**)

E Other clues about Iron Age life

1 Julius Caesar, the Roman general who conquered Gaul (Celtic France) between 59 and 56 BC described how the Gauls would attack a fort: *'They surround the walls with a large number of men and shower it with stones, fired from slings, from all sides, so that the enemy have to keep away from the defences. They then set fire to the gates and undermine the walls.'*

2 A Greek writer living in the first century BC wrote about the Celts of Gaul: *'Instead of the short sword they carry long swords held by iron chains. Some wear gold–plated belts around their tunics. The spears which they use in battle have long iron heads. . . . They cut off the heads of enemies slain in battle and fix them to the necks of their horses. They then nail up these trophies in their houses. They preserve the heads of their most important enemies with cedar oil and display them with pride to strangers.'*

3 A Greek writer in the first century AD wrote: *'The Celts sometimes engaged in single combat at dinner, in a kind of mock battle. But sometimes people were wounded and the anger caused by this sometimes led to the killing of the opponent.'*

4 When Julius Caesar invaded Britain in 55 and 54 BC he noted that the Celts often used iron bars as money.

5 At Butser Hill near Portsmouth archaeologists have rebuilt an Iron Age farm. Storage pits have been filled with grain. If the pits are covered with clay so that they are airtight, most of the grain does not rot and it can be stored for many months.

6 Archaeologists believe that during the last part of the Iron Age the population of Britain was growing and there may have been land shortages.

7 Trade with the Roman Empire was increasing quickly from about 100 BC. Roman goods such as wine, pottery and glass were paid for with metals, leather hides and slaves.

8 Barry Cunliffe writes: *'The dog played an important part in Celtic religion. The Celtic goddess Epona (divine horse) is usually shown seated on a horse, often with a dog by her side. While the raven-god is found time and again in the Celtic stories of Ireland and Gaul.'*

9 In 1984 the body of an Iron Age Man was found preserved in a peat bog in Cheshire. The man had died in about 500 BC by having his throat cut. Archaeologists believe he was a human sacrifice to a god.

4 Oral History: Asking People

How good is your memory? One of the best ways of finding out about the recent past is by asking people about what they can remember. Old people can often tell us a great deal about the changes that have taken place in the lives of ordinary people, as in **A** and **B**:

One night I remember, I'd put five of the kids to bed, washed them and put them in their pyjamas. Then one of the girls comes in about 10 o'clock. I say, "I thought I'd put you to bed". She says "No. I met Mam, and went to the pictures with her". Well a bit later the neighbour comes knocking at the door, she's all upset, "Have you seen our Tommy?" "No, no sign of him." Later on it turns out I've only washed him and put him to bed with ours without noticing. She's that relieved she laughs out loud. "Leave him till morning, he'll not take any harm!" **(A)**

Our mothers were conjurors, they could make a meal out of next to nothing, some bits of offal – of course, they couldn't do it now, it all goes to the factories for pet food . . . At least you could go kebbing (collecting waste coal) *on the tips, you would pick up what the barges dropped by the canal, you could even chop the legs off your chairs, you could burn anything on an open fire . . .* **(B)**

Old people can also tell us about important *events* that have taken place in their lifetimes. For instance, students at Boundstone School in Sussex wanted to find out more about how ordinary people were affected by the Second World War. So they interviewed old people in the local area:

3 September was the day that war was declared. This was a Sunday because I was in church when I heard church bells and air raid sirens sound which meant that war had been declared . . . On 4 September I visited the Oddfellows Hall in Queens Road, Brighton which was used as a recruiting office. I was posted to an RAF station where I was to have my drill training, commonly known as square bashing. This was a bit of a bad time but looking back, it gave me self-confidence, independence and also the ability to get on with all kinds of people . . . **(C)**

I lived in West London . . . First it was just the hassle of blacking out your windows. Then the air raids started to get bigger and bigger. My parents lost their house so they came in with me . . . By now I had lost mine, but all the neighbours were so friendly and we all shared the houses that were left. We had card parties most of the nights . . . Food was rationed but it was the least of our troubles and we always

managed. Where homes had been there were now allotments and people shared their vegetables . . .

The bad times get forgotten, but I shall always remember the kindness and friendliness of everyone during those days . . . **(D)**

Our memories are not always reliable. We don't remember everything. As time goes by we may forget details of things or confuse events. Sometimes we *choose* to forget. Policemen often find that witnesses of accidents or robberies give very different accounts of the same incidents, even though they all believe they are telling the truth.

Problems of memory don't just affect *oral* (spoken) history, they affect nearly every kind of historical evidence. Even so, the historian Paul Thompson points out:

Through drawing on the amazing range of experience held in living memory, oral history offers us a means of looking at the huge changes of our time. At the same time, through their own words, we can share with people of all kinds an understanding of the impact of history on their own lives. **(E)**

??????????????

1 Look at **A** and **B**. In what ways do they suggest life has changed for ordinary people?

2 a In what ways might **A** and **B** be unreliable?
b How did the man in **C** remember that the war began on a Sunday?
c What does the person in **D** tell us about the problems of memory? Are there any signs of this in **A–C**?

3 Class activity Interview old people you know about changes or events during their lifetimes. (Work out the questions you want to ask first.)

To the teacher To demonstrate the problems of memory you could stage an 'incident' in the classroom. Get some older pupils to come in on an errand. Get them to behave in a strange way. Continue with the lesson for 10 minutes or so, then ask the class a series of questions about the incident. This will show how unreliable memory can be.

5 Photographs

A A Victorian family 'at home'

Do you like having your photograph taken? Which photos show what you are really like – those where you are posing for the camera, or those where you are caught off your guard?

The camera was invented by an Englishman called Fox-Talbot in 1841. Early cameras could not take 'snap-shots' or 'action-shots' because they needed a long exposure time. So early photographers required people to keep still, otherwise pictures would be blurred.

Photographs can clearly be an important source of evidence in many different ways, but sometimes the camera can lie!

Family Photographs

Have you got a family photo album? Does it give a true idea of what your family is really like? **A** is a photograph of a wealthy Victorian family. What is there to suggest that they are posing for the camera? We know from other sources that in Victorian times the father was usually the head of the family. He usually took all the decisions. How has the photographer tried to suggest this in **A**?

School Photographs

Have you seen photographs of your parents, grand-parents or great-grandparents when they were at school? **B** shows children at a school in Bradford in 1901. Jot down the things which might suggest that these children come from very poor families. What can we learn from this about what parts of Bradford must have been like in

B Bradford schoolchildren in 1901

C/D RAF fighter pilots relaxing before take-off

1901? What problems do you think these children would have faced in school?

Wartime Photographs

Did your grandparents or any other elderly relatives fight in the Second World War? They may have some old photos of themselves in uniform. **C** and **D** show RAF pilots in 1940, during the Battle of Britain. These pilots were often sent into action five or six times a day. Many lost their lives. What evidence is there in the photos that they are ready for action? Do any of the pilots show signs of being nervous? The pilots in one of these photographs knew that their picture was being taken. Which one? What impression do you get of RAF

pilots during the Battle of Britain from looking at **C**? Which photograph do you think probably gives the more true-to-life picture of what it was like to wait around between missions?

Politics and Photographs

Photographs are very important to politicians. They use them to put over political messages. **E** is a famous photograph. It shows Mao Zedong with a group of young students and teachers. It was taken in the 1960s when Mao Zedong was the leader of Communist China. What idea are we meant to get about Mao from this photograph? How far can we trust it as evidence?

'Fixed' Photographs

Sometimes photographs are 'fixed' in such a way that they are completely misleading. Sometimes this is called 'trick photography'. Look at **F**, **G** and **H**. At least one of the photographs is probably a fake. Which one(s)?

In 1917 there was a Communist revolution in Russia. The men who led the revolution were Lenin and Trotsky. **F** shows Lenin making a speech in 1917 with Trotsky at the edge of the platform (on the right of the photograph). Without Lenin and Trotsky, Russia might never have become a Communist country. In the USSR

E Chairman Mao Zedong with 'revolutionary students and teachers' at the Tienanmen Gate in Beijing

F Lenin addressing a meeting in 1917. Trotsky is standing to the right of the platform

G A drawing showing Lenin (far left) with Stalin sitting beside him

H A photograph of Lenin and Stalin at Gorki in 1922

(Communist Russia) Lenin has always been seen as one of the greatest men that ever lived.

Lenin expected that Trotsky would one day lead the USSR. After Lenin's death in 1924 there was a struggle for power between Trotsky and Stalin, the General Secretary of the Communist Party. Lenin had disliked Stalin, thinking he was a dull man and not very clever. Stalin won the struggle and later expelled Trotsky from the country, calling him an 'enemy of the people'. Stalin then set about re-writing history. Russians were told that it was really Stalin who had been Lenin's right-hand man, not Trotsky. Paintings were produced showing Stalin at Lenin's side rather than Trotsky (see **G**). Photographs of Lenin had Stalin's picture added to them. Look at **H** very carefully. What is there to suggest that this photograph may have been rigged?

So whenever you look at photographs as evidence, ask yourself:

● Why was this photograph taken?
● What does it tell me about the people, places or events shown?
● What can I learn from looking closely at the details in the photograph?
● Does this photograph tell me the truth, or is it simply somebody's point of view?
● Is this photograph misleading or a fake?
● Is this photograph a primary or a secondary source?

15

6 Letters

Letters are very important sources of evidence. Sometimes they give information which is not recorded anywhere else. Of course, people write letters for many different reasons. News letters, love letters, business letters, begging letters, threatening letters and many other types can all be used by historians to piece together what has happened in the past. This chapter looks at three very different letters. The first two were written by quite ordinary people. The third letter was written by a man who made himself the ruler of England. Letters written by such famous people can tell us a great deal about the writer.

A parent's letter

When did your parents or guardian last write a letter to a teacher at your school? Could that letter be of use to historians one day? **A** is a letter written by a parent in 1886 about her children's schooling.

> *Magham Down,*
> *Hailsham,*
> *County of Sussex*
>
> *I now write a few lines to you to ask you if my daughters can leave school I have sent there (their) own writing and there age and figures because we cannt finde them in clothes and food and keep a home for them any longer without there help there father his (is) 60 years of age and he goes 4 miles every morning and 4 miles back that makes 8 miles a day and then if it his fine all the week so he can work on the farm he gets 14s (70p) but if it his not he cannot work on the farm he his paid for the days he does work so his earning never amounts to more than 10s (50p) a week and very often under 10s in the winter months so what can we do if there should be any illnis not a farthing to help ourselves with . . . it his no wonder the farmers do not prosper when they oppress (put down) the labourers has they do and this cruel cruel law of a school board it his too bad we cannot do it because the weather is not warme enuff for them to go without clothes and so they must have clothes and food . . .*
>
> *Mrs Spray* **(A)**

(On the back of the letter Mrs Spray's two 14-year-old daughters gave examples of their neatest writing and also did some sums.)

Mrs Spray wrote her letter in 1886. In 1870 the Education Act had set up school boards throughout Britain. In 1880 schooling became compulsory for the first time in many areas. Parents who wanted their children to leave school early had to get permission. This was only given if past attendance was good and if the children had reached a high enough standard. What clues does this give you about Mrs Spray's letter?

Now think about these points:

- What do we learn about Mrs Spray from this letter?
- What is the purpose of the letter?
- The new schools were very unpopular in many places. Does this letter help explain why?
- What is there in **A** to show that the Spray family is very poor? Who does Mrs Spray blame for this?
- How far can we trust what Mrs Spray says about how poor her family is?

Mrs Spray suggests that many farm workers felt cheated by the farmers they worked for. This was nothing new, as is shown in the next letter.

A threatening letter

Do you find other people's writing difficult to read? This can be a problem for historians when looking at hand-written evidence such as letters. Look at **B**, a letter written in 1830.

Copy it in your own handwriting, then read it out slowly to yourself. This will help you work out what it says. Now think about the answers to these questions:

- What is there to show that the writer is a poor person?
- How has the writer signed his/her name? Why?
- What kind of person/people was this letter written to?
- What is the letter writer demanding?
- What threat does he/she make?

In fact a great many threatening letters like this one were written in 1830 and 1831 in the south of England. They all made the same demands and they were usually signed 'Swing' or signed with a squiggle. The historian Simon Mason tells us:

Ever since 1815 there had been great hardship amongst the farm labourers. Many farmers in the south of England had started to use machines for threshing corn (separating the

B A 'threatening' letter written at the time of the Swing Riots

this is to inform you what you have to undergo Jentelmen if providing you Dont pull down your mesohénes and rise the poor mens wages the maried men give tow and six pence a day a day the singel tow shilings or we will burn down your barns and you in them this is the last notis

from W.W.

grains of corn from the straw). *The labourers saw in them a sign of their misery, so they started to set fire to hay ricks and to destroy the machines. They claimed they were led by a man called Swing, but no one can be certain if he really existed. By 1831 nine men had been hanged for taking part in the Swing Riots and 357 men and boys transported to Australia.* **(C)**

A news letter

When was Northern Ireland last in the news? The 'Troubles' in Ireland have been going on for hundreds of years. **D** is a letter written by Oliver Cromwell, an English Protestant. He describes how on 10 September 1649 he dealt with a Catholic rebellion. At this time Cromwell was the most powerful man in Britain.

● How long after the battle was this letter written? Do you think Cromwell would still be able to remember all the details?

● Although Cromwell was the most powerful man in Britain he did not have the support of all MPs. Many

To the Hon. William Lenthall, Speaker of Parliament of England. Dublin

17th September 1649

Sir,

God has blessed our efforts at Drogheda. We fired our cannons at the town, then we stormed it. There were about 3000 of the enemy.

God gave a new courage to our men; they made another attempt and got in, beating the enemy from their defence. We refused to give mercy to the defenders because the day before we had called on them to surrender and they had refused. I believe we put to the sword (killed) all the defenders.

About 100 enemy officers and soldiers fled into St Peter's Church steeple. When they refused to surrender I ordered the steeple to be set on fire.

Other enemy soldiers had fled into the Round Tower. They too refused to surrender, but we knew that hunger would force them down in the end. From the tower they killed and wounded some of our men. When they finally surrendered, their officers were knocked on the head and every tenth man of the soldiers were killed, and the rest put in prison ships.

I believe that our victory is a judgement by God. And I truly believe that the firmness we have shown will prevent any more blood shed in the future. The enemy expected us to be beaten. But we were not. And why not? It was not done by our power and strength but by the Spirit of God. That is clearly so. And therefore it is good that God alone should have all the glory for this victory.

Yours faithfully,
Oliver Cromwell **(D)**

thought he had too much power. What kind of impression is Cromwell trying to give Parliament about himself and what he has done?

● What can we learn about Cromwell as a person from this letter? Choose the words which you think best describe him: religious, evil, saintly, honest, kind, far-seeing, brave, firm, cruel, stern, strong, weak, fair, wise, humble, boastful, ignorant, stupid, clever, vengeful. Now think up some others of your own.

● If you were English and a Protestant, would you have liked to have lived under Cromwell's rule?

Cromwell said 'the firmness we have shown will prevent any more blood shed in the future.' He could not have been more wrong. Yet it was not until 1922 that British rule ended in most of Ireland. Oliver Cromwell is one of the most hated names in Irish history.

7 Diaries

Do you keep a diary, or know of someone who keeps a diary? What kinds of things could you write in a diary which might be of use to future historians? Diaries can be important sources of evidence. They usually tell us a good deal about the character and way of life of the person who wrote them. They may provide *primary* evidence about important events and people. They can also help us to build up a picture of everyday life at a particular time and place.

People write diaries for many different reasons and this can affect how reliable they are. For instance, politicians sometimes keep diaries which they mean to be published in the future. This may well affect what they write down about themselves and other people, and what they leave out. So as historians, whenever we look at diaries we must ask ourselves:

a Why did this person keep a diary?
b Did he/she mean other people to read it at any time?
c Was the diarist honest about himself/herself and other people?
d How far does the diarist give a complete picture of the things he/she has written about? Are important details left out?
e Was the diarist in a position to know about the things he/she has written about?

A Anne Frank

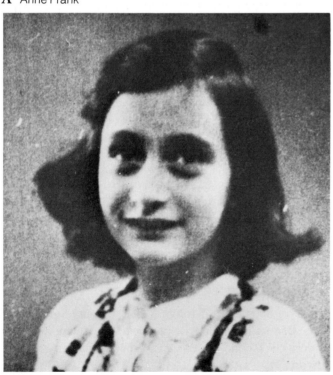

f What do we learn about the diarist as a person from what he/she has written?

This chapter looks at the diary of a teenage girl. Her name was Anne Frank (**A**). (She kept her diary for over two years, so only a very small part of it can be printed on these pages).

The Diary of Anne Frank

Anne was given her diary for her thirteenth birthday. It begins with a dedication.

❝I hope I shall be able to tell you everything, as I have never been able to do to anyone else, and I hope that you will be a great support to me.
(Anne Frank, 12 June 1942)

Saturday 20 June 1942 It seems to me that no one else will be interested in what a 13-year-old schoolgirl has to say. Still, does that matter? I want this diary to be my friend for whom I have waited so long. I shall call my friend Kitty. I will begin my letters to Kitty by sketching my life. My sister Margot was born in Frankfurt (Germany) in 1926 and I followed in 1929. As we are Jewish we moved to Holland in 1933. After May 1940 (when Nazi Germany conquered Holland) our family felt the full impact of Hitler's anti-Jewish laws . . . Jews must wear a yellow star, Jews are banned from trams and are forbidden to drive. Jews are only allowed to do their shopping between 3 and 5 o'clock in shops which have the sign "Jewish Shop". Jews must be indoors by 8 o'clock and cannot even sit in their gardens after that hour. Jews are forbidden to enter places of entertainment, swimming baths, tennis courts, hockey fields and other sports grounds are all barred to them . . .❞ (**B**)

Shortly after this Anne's family went into hiding to escape being sent off to a German concentration camp. They moved into the small Secret Annexe of an old warehouse in Amsterdam. There they were joined by the Van Daan family and by Mr Dussel, so that there were eight of them in all. Four friends of Mr Frank secretly supplied them with food, clothes, books and newspapers.

❝Saturday 11 July 1942 Dear Kitty,
I don't think I shall ever feel really at home in this house, but that does not mean that I hate it here . . . The Secret Annexe is a perfect hiding place . . . I can't tell you how horrible it is never to be able to go outdoors and also I'm very afraid that we shall be discovered and shot . . .

Friday 9 October 1942 *Dear Kitty,*

I've got terrible, depressing news today. Our Jewish friends are being taken away by the dozen. They are loaded into cattle trucks and sent to Westerbork, the Jewish Camp. It is impossible to escape, most of the people in the camp are branded by their shaven heads. The English radio speaks of Jews being gassed . . . Elli (one of their suppliers) is very quiet. Her boyfriend has got to go to Germany. Dirk is not the only one: trainloads of boys leave daily . . .

Wednesday 13 January 1943 *Dear Kitty,*

Everything has upset me again this morning. It is terrible outside. Day and night more of these poor miserable people are being dragged off. Families are torn apart, women and children separated. Children coming home from school find that their parents have disappeared. Women return from shopping to find their homes shut up and their families gone . . . The whole world is waging war, and although it is going better for the Allies the end is not yet in sight. We are luckier than millions of people. It is quiet and safe here.

Tuesday 27 April 1943 *Dear Kitty,*

The air raids on German towns are growing in strength every day. We don't have a single quiet night . . . Our food is miserable. Dry bread and coffee substitute for breakfast. Dinner: spinach or lettuce and small potatoes which taste sweet and rotten.

Thursday 16 September 1943 *Dear Kitty,*

Relations between us are getting worse all the time. At meal times no one dares open their mouths because you either annoy someone or it is misunderstood . . . Everyone looks with fear and terror towards that great terror, winter. Another thing, the warehouse man is becoming suspicious about the Secret Annexe.

Wednesday 29 March 1944 *Dear Kitty,*

A minister speaking on the Dutch news from London said that they ought to make a collection of letters and diaries after the War. But it would seem funny ten years after the war if we Jews were to tell how we lived and what we ate and talked about here. I tell you a lot, even so you know very little of our lives . . .

Thursday 6 April 1944 *Dear Kitty,*

You asked me what my hobbies and interests were. I warn you there are heaps of them. First of all: writing but that hardly counts as a hobby. Two: family trees. I've been searching for the family trees of all the royal families in all the newspapers and books I can find. My third hobby is history. Daddy has already bought me a lot of books. I have a great hatred of maths, geometry and figures.

Tuesday 6 June 1944 *Dear Kitty,*

"This is D-Day", came the announcement over the English news at 8 o'clock this morning . . . The invasion has begun!

The long – awaited liberation! It seems too wonderful, too much like a fairy-tale!

Tuesday 1 August 1944 *Dear Kitty,*

I've told you before that I have two personalities. One half of me is high-spirited, cheerful and the way I take everything lightly. The other side is much deeper. No one knows Anne's better side and this is why most people find me so difficult to get on with. The lighter side always pushes under the better side . . . I'm used to not being taken seriously but only the "light-hearted" side of Anne can bear it, the "deeper" Anne is too frail for it. The bad is on the outside and the good is on the inside, and I keep trying to find a way of becoming what I would so like to be . . . (C)

Anne's diary ends here. On 4 August 1944 the German secret police and Dutch Nazis raided the Secret Annexe. The Frank family, the Van Daans and Mr Dussel were all sent off to concentration camps. The Germans ransacked the Annexe and Anne's diary was left lying on the floor.

During the Second World War over six million Jews were killed by the Nazis. Of the eight members of the Secret Annexe, only Anne's father survived. He was freed by the Russians in 1945. Anne and her sister Margot were sent to Bergen–Belsen Camp where they both died of typhus in March 1945, a few weeks before the end of the War. Anne was 15 years old.

(If you want to read more of *The Diary of Anne Frank* there should be a copy in your school or local library.)

??????????????

1 Write out your answers to points **a** – **f** on page 18.

2 a How did Anne know what was happening to the Jews: before July 1942; after July 1942?
b What is there to suggest that Anne was in some ways lonely despite being with people all the time?
c Look at what Anne says on Tuesday 1 August 1944. In what ways did people who *knew* Anne see her differently from the way we see her through her diary? (Look back at how you answered **f** in question 1.)

3 Anne's father decided to publish her diary in 1947 because he was sure this is what Anne would have wanted. Many people who keep diaries write personal things that they do not mean to be read by anyone else. Do historians have the right to read these things even after the person has died?

4 Can we trust the diary as a reliable source of evidence about Anne Frank and her family?

8 Pictures and Cartoons

A Bishopsgate Street in London: an engraving by Gustav Doré

B 'American Progress'

Drawings and paintings of historical events, people and places can often be more useful than photographs as historical evidence. This is because artists can bring out important details which might be blurred, overlooked or not show up at all on a photograph. For example, look at **A**, a Victorian street scene drawn in 1872.

However, when we look at drawings or paintings we are not simply seeing a picture of 'what happened'. We are seeing somebody's view of what happened. In pictures such as **B** the artist is clearly putting across a political message. **B** was also drawn in 1872 and is called 'American Progress'.

The most common type of pictures that set out to make a political point are political cartoons. Often cartoons are not meant to be funny. Sometimes they are deadly serious. Cartoons can often sum up a whole political point of view in one simple drawing. This is why they are so widely used in newspapers and magazines. **C** is a *Punch* cartoon of 1843, which gives one view of Victorian society.

C 'Capital and Labour'

D 'Sans-Culottes refreshing after the tiring tasks of the day'

E Main events of the French Revolution

In 1789 there was a revolution in France. For hundreds of years the French royal family and the rich nobles had lived in luxury while most ordinary French people were very poor indeed. In 1789 the old order was swept away. The slogan of the Revolution was *'Liberté, Egalité, Fraternité'* which means 'Liberty, Equality and Brotherhood'. A National Assembly was set up to run the country. Most of the nobles were imprisoned and many were beheaded by the guillotine. King Louis XVI found that he had lost all his power.

Under the new government, law and order broke down completely. The rulers of other countries became worried that the revolution might spread so Austrian and Prussian troops invaded France. A Paris mob calling themselves 'Sans Culottes' (see **E**) were determined to defend the Revolution at all costs. In September 1792 they went on the rampage, killing imprisoned nobles and anyone else they thought might be against the Revolution. Thousands lost their lives. Millions of French people lived in terror. In 1793 Louis XVI and his wife Marie Antoinette were executed and France became a republic.

In times of war cartoonists sometimes become openly racialist about an enemy country. D was drawn in September 1792 by Gillray, a British cartoonist. It is about events that were going on in France at the time. It was published just a short time before war broke out between Britain and France. E explains what was happening in France. Does D give a true or a false impression of these events?

Cartoons are often used on posters, too. F is a famous British poster printed during the Second World War. It points to one of the government's biggest worries.

Like other historical sources, cartoons can tell us a good deal about people and events of long ago. Yet in order to properly understand them we need to already know something about those same events and people.

You never know who's listening!

CARELESS TALK COSTS LIVES

F One of a series of posters produced during the Second World War. (The men on the back seat are Hitler and Goering)

??????????????

1 a What can we learn about some streets in Victorian London from **A**? How does the artist show that these people are very poor?

b Describe what is happening in **B**. What point is the artist making? Do you agree with him?

c In **F** the men on the back seat are Hitler and Goering, another leading Nazi. What point is the poster making? Why do many posters and advertisements have funny cartoons on them?

2 a Look at **C** carefully. What does this cartoon tell us about the 'misery of the coalmines'?

b Can we trust **C** as a reliable source of evidence about conditions in the mines?

c What points is the cartoonist making?

3 a What impression is Gillray trying to give of the Sans Culottes in **D**?

b We know that the Sans Culottes were *not* cannibals. Why should Gillray make out that they were?

4 Design a cartoon of your own about some recent event in politics or something that has happened at your school. What value might this cartoon have to a historian in 50 years time?

9 Newspapers

Newspapers are important sources of evidence. But as with all historical sources the problem is: how far can we trust them? Think about these points:

- newspapers take sides
- sometimes they leave out important facts
- they do not always tell the truth
- they exaggerate
- they describe things in a one-sided way
- they try to influence what we think.

This chapter looks at newspaper reports in times of peace and in war time.

NEWSPAPERS IN PEACE TIME

The General Strike 1926

On 4 May 1926 a General Strike began in Britain. It lasted for nine days. In 1925 the owners of the coal mines had decided to cut miners' pay and increase working hours. The mine-owners said this was the only way the mining industry could survive. The miners saw no reason why they should take a cut in pay. The Trades Union Congress (TUC) promised its support to the miners. Millions of people thought the miners were being badly treated.

The Conservative Government, led by Stanley Baldwin, agreed to set up a Royal Commission (government inquiry) to look into the dispute. Meanwhile, the government made plans on how to keep the country going in the event of a general strike. In 1926 the Royal Commission reported that the miners should take pay cuts and accept longer hours.

On 30 April 1926 the miners went on strike. A special TUC conference promised to join in a general strike unless the government and coal mine owners gave way. On 4 May 1926 the General Strike began.

Few newspapers appeared on 4 May. On 5 May the *Daily Mail* reported on what was happening (A).

A *Daily Mail* reports on the General Strike

‘ ## FIRST DAY OF GENERAL STRIKE
FOOD PLANS WORK SMOOTHLY
THOUSANDS OF VOLUNTEERS

Yesterday was the first day of the General Strike. Volunteers for emergency services are registering in large numbers and government plans are running smoothly. Food supplies are normal. The Trades Union Congress, realising that the strike is likely to fail have been making desperate efforts to find grounds for calling it off. The Government is determined that talks cannot be re-started until the general strike has been ended.

STRIKERS' WAR ON PETROL

Thousands of strikers yesterday refused to allow any petrol to leave the London docks. The manager of one petrol company told *Daily Mail* reporter that the strikers had turned the taps on the petrol tanks and allowed thousands of gallons to run down street gutters and drains.

MOB AND A MOTOR CAR

Shortly after midnight on Monday a crowd led by men carrying red flags surrounded a motor car, containing two men and two women, apparently meaning to overturn it. They were dispersed by police. Afterwards they tried to walk in the direction of Buckingham Palace and after several clashes with police they were scattered.

LOOKING TO MR BALDWIN TO ACT

On Sunday evening the *Daily Mail* was prevented by printers from being published because we called on the people to stand by King and Country. On Monday evening printers stopped nearly all the evening papers and once more the *Daily Mail* did not come out. They did not print the *Daily Mail* because it called for the arrest at once of the leaders of the plot against the freedom of the British nation . . .

The British nation is eager to support its Government. It is waiting for its Government to act. When a fight is in progress (and the leaders of this strike have not hesitated to use the word ‘war') the only thing to do is to win it, not to think of what will happen if we do not win it. The lawful government must act strongly and its opponents will collapse very quickly. Half of them hate this general strike with its terrible cruelty to the weak and poor who are always the worst sufferers through their violence.

Here is the leading story from Monday's *Daily Mail* which the printers refused to print:

FOR KING AND COUNTRY!

. . . We do not wish to say anything hard about the miners themselves. As to their leaders all we need say is that some of them are (and have openly declared themselves) under the influence of people who mean no good to this country. A general strike is not an industrial dispute. It is a movement for revolution aimed at making masses of innocent people suffer . . . We call on all law – abiding men and women to put themselves at the service of King and Country.

FOOD TRANSPORT

Within a few hours of the Government's emergency supply services being in operation they were running with smoothness and efficiently. The railway plans for the use of volunteer labour worked well. ’ (A)

THE
BRITISH WORKER
OFFICIAL STRIKE NEWS BULLETIN
Published by The General Council of the Trades Union Congress

No. 1. | WEDNESDAY EVENING, MAY 5, 1926. | PRICE ONE PENNY

IN LONDON AND THE SOUTH

Splendid Loyalty of Transport Workers

EVERY DOCKER OUT

" London dock workers are absolutely splendid," said an official of the Transport and General Workers' Union.

" So far as they are concerned, it is a 100 per cent. strike. There is no trouble and everything is going smoothly."

WONDERFUL RESPONSE TO THE CALL

General Council's Message : Stand Firm and Keep Order

The workers' response has exceeded all expectations. The first day of the great General Strike is over. They have manifested their determination and unity to the whole world. They have resolved that the attempt of the mineowners to starve three million men, women and children into submission shall not succeed.

SOUTH WALES IS SOLID !

Not a Wheel Turning in Allied Industries

'MEN ARE SPLENDID !'

Throughout South Wales the stoppage is complete, and everywhere the men are loyally observing the orders of the T.U.C. to retrain from any conduct likely to lead to disturbance.

So unanimous has been the response to the call of the leaders, that

B Front page of *The British Worker*, 5 May 1926

During the General Strike the TUC printed its own newspaper *The British Worker*. **B** shows the front page of *The British Worker* on 5 May 1926.

C shows the front page of the *British Gazette* on 8 May 1926. It was an official government newspaper, edited by Winston Churchill, the Chancellor of the Exchequer.

C Front page of *The British Gazette*, 8 May 1926

PLEASE PASS ON THIS COPY OR DISPLAY IT

The British Gazette
Published by His Majesty's Stationery Office.

No. 4. | LONDON, SATURDAY, MAY 8, 1926. | ONE PENNY.

ORGANISED ATTEMPT TO STARVE THE NATION

Orders By Leaders Of The Railway And Transport Trade Unions.

SUBSTANTIAL IMPROVEMENT IN THE TRAIN SERVICES.

Government's New Steps To Protect The People.

SITUATION BECOMING MORE INTENSE.

OFFICIAL COMMUNIQUE.

May 7.

No serious disorder has occurred in any part of the country. The work of feeding the people and of maintaing light and power and essential communications is being successfully accomplished. Over

FALSE NEWS.

Printer And Street Sellers in Court.

A WARNING.

Prompt Action By The Police.

The public are advised to pay no attention to alarmist rumours which may be spread by disaffected persons. Typical cases are the circulation of such reports as that the Post Office Savings Bank has suspended payment, and that mutinies have occurred among his Majesty's Forces. Such reports are wholly untrue. Their circulation is a criminal offence.

This notification, which appeared in the official communique in Thursday's *British Gazette*, had a sequel when the printer and sellers of a leaflet containing false news of the Liverpool police having come out on strike appeared at the Marylebone Police Court.

Henry William Adlem, of 3, Salestreet, Paddington, was charged with committing an act likely to cause disaffection among the civil population of Great Britain."

Detective-inspector Brust, of the Special Branch of Scotland Yard, described

The folowing announcement is made by his Majesty's Government:

All ranks of the Armed Forces of the Crown are hereby notified that any action which they may find it necessary to take in an honest endeavour to aid the Civil Power will receive, both now and afterwards, the full support of his Majesty's Government.

CREWS FOR LINERS.

Volunteer Dockers Busy At Liverpool.

Southampton Sailings.

A return to normal shipping conditions is gradually bring made, both at Liverpool and Southampton.

The position at Liverpool has improved to such an extent that eighteen vessels docked and ten undocked on Thursday. Volunteer labour continues to pour in, and on Friday sixteen vessels were being discharged. The work

FOURTH DAY IN THE PROVINCES.

Tendency to Return In Some Industries.

870 Engineers Back at Leeds.

Exciting Level-Crossing Scene.

The outstanding feature of the latest reports from the provinces is the indication of a desire to return to work in many industries. For instance, 870 engineers have already gone back in Leeds, 70 out of 200 co-operative workers have returned at Pendleton, and 50 transport workers have resumed in the Halifax district.

NORTH-EASTERN DIVISION.

The West Riding is reported quiet. Essential services are maintained, and railways an droad transport are improving. Fifty transport workers returned to dut yin Halifax and 700 engineers at Armley and 170 at Pudsey went back to work. Large supplies of fish went to London by road.

Independent 'buses have restarted at Hull, and 57 trains and 'buses were running in Leeds on Thursday. Forty trains passed through Doncaster on Thursday. A large number of men in the building trade have ceased work at Bradford, but there has been discussion at labour meetings, and there is some talk of a return to work.

LORD OXFORD AND ASQUITH'S MESSAGE.

British People On The Rack.

STRIKE WEAPON AIMED AT DAILY LIFE OF THE COMMUNITY.

Must Be Sheathed Before Negotiations.

There could be no greater misunderstanding of the attitude of our people at this moment than to suppose that it implies any hostility to the right of combination in industry. Strikes and lock-outs, though they always inflict a certain amount of inconvenience on the public, may be, and often are, in the last resort justifiable and even necessary. But the challenge which has now been thrown down and taken up is of a totally different kind.

A General Strike, such as that which it is being sought to enforce, is directly aimed at the daily life of the whole community. The people who suffer least from it are the capitalists and the plutocrats. They have at their command the whole apparatus of opulence, and the petty discomforts to which they are exposed are not more than pin-

Stanley Baldwin also used the BBC to put over the government's message. No right to reply was given to the strike leaders. Baldwin said in a radio broadcast; 'I am a man of peace. I am longing and working and praying for peace'. He promised that if the strike was ended, returning workers would not be picked on. TUC leaders were prepared to believe him. They were worried that the Strike could lead to a complete breakdown in government. On 12 May the General Strike was called off. However, many strikers found that on their return to work they were made to suffer at the hands of their bosses. Many were forced to take pay cuts. In 1927 Parliament passed the Trades Disputes Act, making general strikes illegal. The miners fought on alone for six months, until they were starved back to work for even lower wages. Many miners still feel bitter about what happened in 1926.

NEWSPAPERS IN WARTIME

Newspapers written during wartime are even less reliable as sources of evidence. Many newspaper reporters and editors see it as their duty to support the war effort. They become more one-sided. They often write a lot about the good news and say little about the things that go wrong. Reports from the battle front may be censored. Reporters often find that governments and generals keep the facts from them, for fear of giving information away to the enemy. Reporters who are critical of the war effort may be seen as 'traitors'.

The First Battle of the Somme 1916

D shows extracts from the front page of the *News of the World* for 2 July 1916. By this time the First World War had been going on for nearly two years. Since the winter of 1914 the fighting had been at stalemate. The historian Barry Bates tells us:

❝*In the autumn of 1914 both sides began to dig trenches to protect their armies during the winter. The generals thought that in the spring open warfare would begin again. They were proved wrong, for once the line of trenches was dug it proved hard for an army to break through. All attempts meant huge numbers of dead and wounded soldiers. A line of trenches stretched right across Western Europe and altered little during the four years of war.*❞ **(E)**

On 1 July 1916 British General Douglas Haig tried to break the stalemate, with an all-out attack on the German trenches. Look at the *News of the World* stories shown in **D**. Jot down what they tell you about each of the following:

- the success of the attack
- preparations for the attack
- German losses
- British losses

- how the war seems to be going

In fact, 1 July 1916 was the worst day in the history of the British Army. German soldiers survived the shelling before the attack; they were deep underground, with all the food they needed. So when the British troops went 'over the top' of their trenches they were mown down by machine gun fire. 20 000 British troops were killed and another 40 000 wounded on this first day of the attack. (The battle went on until November.) Few German trenches were taken and held.

British soldiers on leave found that the people at home knew little of what the fighting was really like. They seemed to support the war much more than the soldiers did. Siegfried Sassoon, a British officer, wrote this poem:

❝*I knew a simple soldier boy*
Who grinned at life in empty joy,
Slept soundly through the lonesome dark
And whistled early with the lark.

In winter trenches, cowed and glum,
With crumps and lice and lack of rum,
He put a bullet through his brain.
No one spoke of him again.

You smug faced crowds with kindling eye,
Who cheer when soldier lads march by,
Sneak home and pray you'll never know,
The hell where youth and laughter go.❞ **(F)**

Many people thought Sassoon was a traitor for writing this.

German people seem to have had even less idea about what was happening at the front, as is shown on pages 34–35.

D

BRITISH ADVANCE

16 MILES OF GERMAN FRONT TRENCHES STORMED

'The Day Goes Well' for our Heroic Troops.

Special Telegrams to the *News of the World*.

British Headquarters, July 1 – Attack launched north of the River Somme this morning at 7.30 am in conjunction with French.

British troops have broken into German forward system of defence on front of 16 miles.

Fighting is continuing.

French attack on our immediate right proceeding equally satisfactorily.

On remainder of British front raiding parties again succeeded in penetrating enemy's defences at many points, inflicting loss on enemy and taking some prisoners.

News to hearten the soul of the nation and inspire it with the highest hopes is contained in the despatch from British Headquarters given above.

Over a front of 16 miles north of the Somme the British have stormed the German front line trenches, and Sir Douglas Haig reports that a great battle is raging on the ground to which our gallant troops have penetrated.

On the immediate right of the British the French also attacked with equally satisfactory results.

Various points of tactical importance have been occupied, including Serre and Montauban. Further south the French have occupied Curlu.

The depth of the advance varies from one to three miles. Of far more consequence than any mere gain of ground is the work of inflicting upon the enemy heavier losses than those he inflicts upon us. When the enemy has had his fill of punishment he must yield ground.

BIG BATTLE RAGING.

BRITISH OCCUPY ENEMY'S FRONT LINES.

Assault Preceded by Terrific Gun Fire.

At grips at last with the enemy on a grand scale, our matchless infantry are giving a glorious account of themselves.

The following telegrams from British Headquarters add many welcome details to Sir Douglas Haig's message given above.

British Headquarters, France, July 1 – At about 7.30 this morning a rigorous attack was launched by the British Army.

The front extends over about 20 miles north of the Somme.

The assault was preceded by a terrific bombardment lasting about 1½ hours.

It is too early as yet to give anything but the barest particulars, as the fighting is developing in intensity, but British troops have already occupied the German front line.

Many prisoners have already fallen into our hands, and as far as can be ascertained our casualties have not been heavy.
Reuter

HOW WE PREPARED.

FLOODS OF FIRE FROM OUR GUNS.

Dashing Raids all Along Line.

For a full week we have deluged the German lines with our artillery fire in preparation for the infantry advance. The terrible effect of the British fire has been described from day to day by special correspondents at British Headquarters, whose accounts appear elsewhere. All agree that nothing to equal it has ever occurred before on the British front. Our curtain fire had been so effective that the Germans were unable to send food to the front line, with the result that the men in some places had been starving for three days . . .

THE DAY GOES WELL.

GALLANT ACHIEVEMENTS OF BRITISH TROOPS.

Capture of Important Points.

British Headquarters, France, July 1, 1.15 pm – Our troops are making good progress into the enemy territory beyond the front line.

We have taken Serre and Montauban, two important tactical points respectively to south-east of Heebuterno and north-east of Broy.

Our troops are fighting in the villages of Mametz and Contalmaison, parts of which they hold.

Our troops are fighting in a most gallant manner, and many prisoners have been taken in the front lines.

The French are advancing on our right with great steadiness and gallantry, and, after the assault, very quickly covered 1¼ miles beyond the enemy front line, capturing Curlu and Faviers Wood.

So far the day goes well for England and France.

???????????????????????????????????

1 What differences are there in the way *The Daily Mail* and the *British Worker* report on the strike? How would you account for these differences?

2 a Look at **C**. What words are used in the headlines to turn the reader against the strike?
b Why do you think **B** and **C** were called the *British* Worker and the *British* Gazette?

3 Where do you think the *News of the World* (**D**) got its information from? What do we learn about General Haig from the newspaper reports?

4 a Why do you think Sassoon wrote poem **F**?
b Why did most people at home not know how terrible the fighting was?
c For what reason might the British government want to stop them knowing?

5 Look at one of today's newspapers. How might a historian find it useful in 100 years time? What problems would he or she face in using it?

10 Biographies

The third car was the President's. He took his usual rear seat alongside his wife. As the motorcade neared downtown Dallas the crowds at the curb became larger . . . Now people were everywhere, waving from office buildings, filling the streets, cheering . . . The President was waving to the crowds. Suddenly there were three shots. The President clutched his neck with both hands and slumped down in his seat. (A)

(from *JFK: The Presidency of John F Kennedy* by Herbert S Parmet)

The three shots were fired by Lee Harvey Oswald on 22 November 1963. Since then, several biographies have been written, telling the life story of the President. Biographies are useful *secondary* sources for the historian.

Biographers often spend years doing research before they start to write down a person's life story. However, like all historical sources, biographies must be used with care. When we look at them we must ask questions:

● *Why has this biography been written?* Biographers are often one-sided. In many cases the biographer has written the book because he or she admires the person. Biographers usually try to see things from the point of view of the person they are writing about. So even where a biographer starts off trying to be unbiased he or she may end up defending everything the person did.

● *Did the biographer know the person he/she has written about?* In many cases a person's biography may be written hundreds of years after their death. In other cases biographers were friends or colleagues of the person they have written about.

● *Has the biographer told the whole story?* Sometimes biographies leave out certain details for lack of space. TV or film biographies are very unreliable. They often cut out or change important events in order to make the story more interesting.

● *Did the biographer have all the sources he/she needed?* Biographers, like other historians, cannot always be sure about what happened. Sometimes they have to write down what seems most likely to have happened.

The sources on these pages are extracts from some of the biographies of John F Kennedy. They describe him at different stages of his Presidency.

Becoming President

When John Kennedy had been sworn in as President on 20 January 1961 he said in his first speech as President:

The torch has been passed to a new generation of Americans . . . Let every nation know that we shall pay any price, bear any burden, meet any hardship, support any friend, oppose any foe to assure the survival and the success of liberty (freedom) . . . And so my fellow Americans: ask not what your country can do for you — ask what you can do for your country. (B)

Rose Kennedy tells us in *Times to Remember*:

Jack's was one of the great Inaugural (swearing in) Addresses in the history of the Republic. I was proud, thankful and humble. I felt that Joe and I had given our country a young President whose words, manners, ideas, character, everything about him spoke of future greatness. (C)

Cuba

In 1959 there was a Communist takeover in Cuba and Fidel Castro became the new ruler. There was now a Communist country only 90 miles from the American coast. In 1961 President Kennedy supported an attempt by Cuban exiles to re-take the island. The attempt was a disaster. William Manchester wrote in his biography of Kennedy, *One Brief Shining Moment*:

. . . The attack by Cuban exiles had been planned by the CIA (US Secret Service) and Kennedy gave it the green light, thus committing the biggest blunder of his career. The exiles were poorly trained and badly armed. Castro's troops outnumbered them 143 to 1. After less than three days the survivors were rounded up, given a show trial and then led off to prison . . . Kennedy blew the whistle on the adventure and made a public statement accepting all blame for the disaster. Actually of course, Eisenhower (the previous President) was responsible for a large part of it. He had ordered the training of the Cuban rebels and had urged Kennedy to carry the idea forward . . . As evidence of the disaster mounted, the President, alone with his wife, broke down and cried. (D)

Herbert S Parmet tells us:

The disaster was Kennedy's. The operation was launched and failed because John Kennedy not only believed those around him but wanted to believe they were right. (E)

In 1962 there was another Cuban Crisis. A US spy plane discovered that the Russians were building nuclear missile sites in Cuba. Kennedy took firm action and on 22 October 1962 set up a naval blockade of Cuba. Any ship entering the *exclusion zone* (the area inside the blockade) would be sunk. This included Russian ships heading towards Cuba. Herbert S Parmet has written:

G President John F Kennedy and his wife Jackie, in 1960

(Jack's father) *stopped them short: "You're not to speak like that any more . . . Forget all the things you know about Jack's private life. From now on you've got to watch everything you say. The day is coming when he won't be "Jack" any more, he'll be "Mr President".* **(J)**

Conclusions

Edmund Ions has written:

The Presidency of John F Kennedy will be remembered . . . for the leadership and sense of purpose that he gave to Americans. Others reaped what he had sown. The great tributes to him following his death showed that the youngest President in American history had inspired not only the vast majority of Americans but people in all walks of life throughout the world. **(K)**

Herbert Parmet gives a different view:

He had vowed to get America moving again, but failed to deliver in key ways. Glamour overshadowed quality. At best he was an in-between President who had promised but not performed. He gave a new style to the Presidency, one of national pride and hope. That made his limitations all the more painful. **(L)**

There was hardly anyone unaffected by the Cuban Missiles Crisis. Kennedy impressed more than a handful of those who saw him up close during those days with his self-control, his ability to hold a conversation without showing the slightest bit of anxiety. In much of America people braced themselves for disaster . . . **(F)**

Kennedy's tough action worked. In the end the Russian leader Krushchev backed down. He ordered the Russian ships carrying missile equipment to turn back.

Private life

In 1953 John Kennedy married Jacqueline Bouvier, whose looks, intelligence and charm seemed to millions of Americans to make her the perfect 'First Lady'. John and Jackie appeared to be completely devoted to each other **(G)**. Yet some of Kennedy's biographers give a different picture of their marriage. Peter Collier and David Horowitz wrote in *The Kennedys*:

Shortly after the marriage (Jackie) *had said: "I don't think there are many men who are faithful to their wives." However she was not prepared for how great his womanising would be . . . He arranged to meet young women at an apartment hideout . . . Jackie heard about it all.* **(H)**

Collier and Horowitz give us a clue as to why this was not public knowledge at the time:

Lem Billings, an old school friend, remembered an evening in 1957 when he had made a joke about one of Jack's sexual conquests. As Jack and Lem began to laugh old Joe Kennedy

??????????????

1 a One of the sources on these pages is, in fact, from an *auto*biography (someone writing about their own life). Which one do you think it is?
b William Manchester's biography is called *One Brief Shining Moment* **(D)**. What does this tell us about his views on John Kennedy?
c Who does Manchester blame for the Cuban disaster **(D)**?
d Who does Herbert Parmet blame **(E)**?
e How else does Manchester try to defend Kennedy in **D**?

2 Edmund Ions tells us that there were 'great tributes to him following his death'. Yet within a few years JFK's presidency was being severely criticised. This seems to happen to famous politicians a lot. For a while after their deaths they are greatly admired. Then there is often a period when they are attacked (another good example is Winston Churchill). There are clues in this chapter as to why this happens:
a Look at **J**. Why didn't people know much about Kennedy's private life while he was President?
b Why might friends and colleagues be prepared to talk more openly in the years after his death?

3 Have *I* been biased in anything I have written on these pages?

11 Government Documents

A Using government records as historical evidence

Speeches In Britain everything said in Parliament is reported in *Hansard*, a record of Parliament's proceedings. In speeches politicians are usually trying to persuade people round to their point of view. This means they may exaggerate, leave out important points and sometimes say things they don't really mean.

Memoranda and minutes of government meetings. These are usually a short account of what went on over hours of talking. In Britain they are normally kept secret for 30 years. Minutes about defence matters are often kept for much longer under the Official Secrets Act. Governments have sometimes been accused of 'losing' files that might one day embarrass them. This means that historians can never be sure that they are being given the whole story.

Parliamentary reports Sometimes committees of MPs are set up to investigate a problem and report on what they find. The people who make the reports often have strong views. They may want to influence what action the government takes. This can make their reports one-sided.

What do you think of the Government? Are there any politicians who really get on your nerves? Of course, politicians, most of all those in the Government, can play a big part in making history. So as historians we often need to make use of government documents. These include laws, treaties, speeches made in Parliament (in Britain), minutes of meetings, Parliamentary reports, memoranda and a wide range of other sources. All of these must be used with care. **A** shows some of the problems involved.

Despite these drawbacks, government records and reports often give us the kind of *detailed* evidence we are looking for, as the following example shows:

Child Labour

In the first part of the nineteenth century millions of children in Britain worked in factories and mines (see **B**). The work was often dangerous. They worked for long hours for very low pay. In 1832 Parliament set up a committee chaired by Michael Sadler to look into the problem. The committee interviewed 89 people. **C** is part of the *Sadler Report*:

❝Joseph Hebergam, *aged 17 worked in spinning factories at Huddersfield since he was seven:*
"When I had worked about half a year my knees became very weak and it got worse and worse. In the mornings I could hardly walk. My brother and sister used to take me under each arm and run with me to the mill. My legs dragged along the ground because they were so painful. I could not walk. If we were five minutes late the overlooker would take a strap and beat us until we were black and blue."
"Were you once a straight and healthy boy?"
"Yes I was as straight and healthy as anyone when I was seven."
"Your mother being a widow and having but little, could not afford to take you away?"
"No."
"Was she made unhappy by seeing that you were getting crooked and deformed?"
"I have seen her weep sometimes and I have asked her why she was weeping. She would not tell me then but she has told me since . . ."

Elizabeth Bentley, *age 23, lives at Leeds, began work at the age of 6 in Mr Busk's flax mill. Hours were often as long as 5 am to 9 pm with 40 minutes for a meal at noon.*
"Does the work keep you constantly on your feet?"
"Yes there are so many frames (machines) and they run so quick."
"Is your work very exhausting?"
"Yes – you don't have enough time."
"Have you ever been strapped?"
"Yes."
"Were the girls so badly beaten as to leave marks on their skins?"
"Yes, they have had black marks many a time and their parents dared not complain about it because they were afraid of losing their work."
"If the parents were to complain about their children being so badly treated, the child would probably be sacked?"
"Yes."
"Did the work affect your health?"
"Yes, it was so dusty. The dust got into my lungs and the work was so hard. I was quite strong when I went there, but the work was so hard that when I pulled baskets down I pulled my bones out of their places."
"You are very much deformed as a result of the labour?"
"Yes I am."
"When did this happen?"
"I was about 13 years old and it has got worse since my mother died."
"Where do you live now?"
"In the poorhouse at Hunslet."
"You are now quite unable to do any work of that sort?"
"Yes."
"Say what you think of the cruelty and hardship of the work you had to do?"
(The witness was too overcome to answer the question.)❞ **(C)**

B Factory children going to work, 1814

Sadler wanted Parliament to pass a law banning all children under nine from working in the factories and to limit the work of other young people to ten hours a day. He said in the House of Commons in 1832:

❝The Bill (proposed law) *aims to liberate children employed in the factories of the UK. Those who are strongly against this Bill pretend that it is wrong for Parliament to interfere . . . in the relations between employers and their workers. They say that it is wrong to try to regulate the labour market (ie to control the conditions of workers). Some will suggest that children and their parents are free to choose for themselves whether to work in such places. This argument carries little force. The parents who surrender their children to this slavery are for the most part those who are forced to because they are so poor – themselves perhaps out of work or working at very low wages. What else can they do? The parents see their children droop and sicken, and in many cases become cripples and die. It is a choice between this and starvation! Free to choose! To suppose that they freely choose to doom their own flesh and blood to this fate is to believe that they are monsters! . . . The overworking of these children makes them very weary – so exhausted, the poor creatures fall too often into the machines which in many cases are not properly guarded. Their muscles are ripped apart, their bones broken or their limbs torn off . . .* ❞ (**D**)

In 1833 Sadler lost his seat in Parliament at the general election. But his Committee's research had made MPs more aware of the size of the problem. The historian E Royston Pike points out:

❝*Critics have said that some of the evidence was biased, sometimes not accurate and even deliberately misleading!* ❞ (**E**)

In 1833 Lord Ashley managed to get Parliament to pass a Factory Act. This banned children under nine from working in textile factories and made a few other small changes. Even so, many MPs fiercely opposed the Law. It took a series of laws between 1842 and 1878 to really begin to deal with the problem of child labour.

??????????????????

1 a In what ways did child factory workers suffer during the early nineteenth century (**C**, **D**)?
b Why did parents allow their children to do such work (**D**)?
c **B** is a picture of factory children in Yorkshire on their way to work in 1814. What impression is the artist trying to give?
d Can we trust **B** as a source of evidence?

2 a How does the Sadler Report try to get the sympathy of the reader for Joseph and Elizabeth (**C**)?
b Read **E** again. Why might Sadler wish to mislead MPs in his report?
c How far can we trust **D** as a source of evidence?

3 What reasons seem to have been put forward against laws being passed that dealt with child labour and working conditions? What sorts of people might have been against the laws?

4 a As though you are an MP in 1833, draw up a Bill of your own to deal with the problems shown in **C** and **D**. What arguments would you expect some MPs to make against your bill?
Or
b Write a speech of your own attacking child labour.

12 Local Records

Most historians are 'local historians'. They are interested in finding out about the history of the area in which they live. Huge numbers of historical documents are kept at your County Record Office. Most of them have never been studied by historians. They include parish registers, wills, inventories (lists of people's belongings), maps, court records, title deeds, local newspapers, school log books and many other sources. These are vital to historians in piecing together the history of different towns, villages, and cities, and for tracing the 'roots' of individual people – both famous people and ordinary people.

This chapter looks at how local records can be used to find out more about the area in which you live:

- What was this area like 50, 100, 200 or more years ago?
- Who lived here and what were they like?
- What jobs did they do?
- Who did they know?
- What were their homes like?
- How big were their families?
- How long did they live?

The evidence on these pages is about Lancing on the Sussex coast, which is where I teach. Look at maps **A** and **B** inside the back cover. Map **A** is part of an Ordnance Survey map of 1980. A local historian R Kerridge, writes: *'It is a popular seaside resort in the summer and there are direct links by road and rail with Worthing three miles to the west and Brighton eight miles to the east.'* Lancing is called a 'village' but about 20 000 people live there. It is part of a large built-up area which stretches along the south coast for over 25 miles.

Maps

One simple way in which you can find out about how your local area has changed is by looking at old maps. Map **C** on this page shows that if we go back just 100 years or so, Lancing seems to have been very different. Compare it with **A**, then quickly jot down three ways in which the area seems to have changed since 1879 (when **C** was drawn). If we go back to the beginning of the nineteenth century we find that the south coast was not built-up at all. In 1813 it was just a series of villages and a few small towns, as map **B** (at the back of the book) shows.

Place names can also give clues about the past. *Ing* is an old Saxon word meaning 'people'. It was used by the

C Lancing in 1879

irst Saxons to settle in Britain in the fifth century. So
here have probably been settlements at Worth*ing*,
Sompt*ing*, and Lanc*ing* for at least 1500 years. 'Sompt'
comes from the Saxon word *sumpt* meaning 'bog' or
'marsh'. So Lancing was once on the edge of a marsh.

Parish registers

Registers have been kept in most parishes since 1538.
Some go back before this time. In them, the local vicar
recorded the baptisms, marriages and burials that were
carried out by the Church of England in the parish.
Although parish registers are extremely useful we have
to read them with care. They can be a bit confusing.

D and E are from the Lancing Register of Burials. D
shows some of the entries in the register for the year
1813. E gives all the entries between 1818 and 1822,
and a few of the entries between 1823 and 1870.

Most of the people at your school can expect to live
into their mid-70s. How many of the people buried
between 1818 and 1822 (E) were over 70? On average,
people in Britain are living longer than ever before.
Historians point out that people living in past centuries
died much younger. But how do they know this? Parish
registers are one source of evidence. Just by glancing at
E you will notice how young many people were when
they died. To get a rough idea of how long people in the
early nineteenth century could expect to live, work out
the average age of people who were buried in Lancing in
the years 1818–22. (Use a calculator to add up the total
number of years and divide this by the total number of
people.)

D Entries in the Lancing Register of Burials, 1813

Name.	Abode.	When buried.	Age.	By whom the Ceremony was performed.
Thomas Sanders No. 1.	*N. Lancing.*	*29 March 1813*	*55*	*Mr Feilde, Vicar of Lancing*
Mary Hodghinson No. 2.	*Servant of Sir Henry Philp Hotphton S. Lancing.*	*21 June 1813*	*40*	*Mrs Feilde Vicar of Lancing*
Richd Hollingdale. No. 3.	*N. Lancing*	*31 July 1813*	*19*	*Mr Feilde Vicar.*
Mary Ann Martin No. 4.	*Died in a Barn of the Small-pox*	*5 Augt 1813*	*17 Months*	*Mr Feilde Vicar.*

E Burials in Lancing 1818–22

1818

No.	Name	Abode	When Buried	Age
45.	John Steel	South Lancing	23 February	1 day
46.	Ann Hollingdale	North Lancing	13 April	63
47.	Catherine Steel	South Lancing	12 June	67
48.	James Piper	North Lancing	4 July	21
49.	Ann Swift	North Lancing	20 October	18
50.	John Piper	North Lancing	31 October	6
51.	George Piper	Cokeham	14 November	19 mths

1819

No.	Name	Abode	When Buried	Age
52.	Martha Steere	Lancing	24 January	43
53.	Ann Pullen	South Lancing	31 March	33
54.	Richard Sharp	North Lancing	8 April	67
55.	Ann Pullen	South Lancing	16 June	2
56.	Jane Carver	Monks Farm	22 June	3 days
57.	Ann Parsons	Cokeham	25 July	15 mths
58.	Mary Ford	New Shoreham	12 November	81

1820

No.	Name	Abode	When Buried	Age
59.	Amy Hacker	Lancing	14 January	50
60.	Jane Souten	Lancing	23 January	66
61.	Caroline Taylor	Lancing	7 March	30
62.	John Ford	Lancing	24 March	32
63.	Edward Longley	Lancing	28 March	82
64.	John Stepney	Lancing	1 May	42
65.	Samuel Piper	Lancing	7 May	4
66.	Betsy Newman	Lancing	1 June	43
67.	Henrietta Heather	West Grinstead	13 August	32

1821

No.	Name	Abode	When Buried	Age
68.	Thomas Lidbetter	Lancing	February	72
69.	Elizabeth Piper	Lancing	18 March	22
70.	Elizabeth Ives	Lancing	18 March	64
71.	Sarah Swift	Lancing	12 April	77
72.	James Allin	London	22 April	40
73.	Luke Piper	North Lancing	17 June	3 mths
74.	Ellen Ellis Swift	North Lancing	25 June	3
75.	Betty Graves	North Lancing	16 September	13
76.	Caroline Hollingdale	South Lancing	10 October	2 yrs 9 mths
77.	Thomas Miller	North Lancing	28 November	48
78.	Thomas Neville	South Lancing	16 December	21

1822

No.	Name	Abode	When Buried	Age
79.	Edward Langley	North Lancing	10 March	82
80.	William Barham	South Lancing	10 March	9 mths
81.	William	South Lancing	14 June	29
82.	Mary Spicer	South Lancing	7 July	18
83.	Mary Piper	North Lancing	21 July	46
84.	John Gomery William Harwood James Tate	Accidently killed by the falling in of a chalk pit.	1 August	17 16 10
85.	Jane Gobel	South Lancing	13 October	26
86.	Elizabeth Coleman	Brighton	10 November	10 mths
87.	Caroline Gobel	South Lancing	17 November	2 yrs 8 mths
88.	Jane Gobel	South Lancing	25 November	18 mths
89.	Anne Winton	South Lancing	25 November	48
90.	Elizabeth Knight	North Lancing	29 December	82

Other entries in the register include:

No.	Name	Abode	When Buried	Age
99.	William Kimber	North Lancing	6 November 1823	2
117.	Charlotte Cussans	North Lancing	13 April 1825	38
135.	Lucy Cussans	North Lancing	21 December 1826	16
137.	William Page	Lancing	8 February 1827	3
139.	Charlotte Grinyer	Lancing	21 May 1827	10 wks
146.	Mary Kimber	Lancing	19 February 1828	8
165.	Sarah Kimber	Lancing	17 May 1829	13
181.	Jane Kimber	Lancing	27 June 1830	7
232.	Jane Sharpe	Worthing	23 January 1836	17
255.	Elizabeth Kimber	Lancing	16 August 1836	15
465.	William Martin	Lancing	30 July 1851	34
642.	Robert Martin	Lancing	21 October 1864	44
739.	James Martin	Lancing	16 December 1870	49

Of course, this register only tells us for certain about people in Lancing. What do historians need to do to make a better estimate of how long people in Britain as a whole could expect to live in the early nineteenth century? Think about these points:

● Would you expect people in villages such as Lancing to have longer or shorter lives than people in the growing industrial cities (such as Manchester, Liverpool, London, Glasgow and Newcastle)?

● Entry No 4 in D suggests one reason why many people used to die so young. What other reasons can you think of?

F Entries in the Lancing Register of Baptisms 1814–23

No.	When Baptised	Child's Christian Name	Parents Names	Trade
		1814		
22.	5 June (privately baptised)	*Frances* b. 3 June	William & Charlotte *Cussans*	Labourer
26.	21 Aug.	*Jane* b. 1 July	Illegitimate daughter of Sarah *Sayers*	Servant
		1815		
37.	30 April	*Henry* b. 24 Mar.	James & Sarah *Page*	Labourer
43.	17 Sept.	*Sarah* b. 15 Aug.	Thomas & Jane *Kimber*	Labourer
44.	26 Nov.	*Frances* b. 5 Nov.	William & Charlotte *Cussans*	Labourer
45.	24 Dec.	*Samuel* b. 2 Oct.	John & Mary *Piper*	Labourer
		1817		
65.	19 Jan.	*John* b. 12 Dec.	Thomas & Jane *Kimber*	Labourer
68.	25 May	*George* b. 31 April	James & Eliz. *Piper*	Labourer
75.	2 Nov.	*Ann* b. 7 Sept.	George & Ann *Pullen*	Butcher
		1818		
78.	28 Feb.	*William* b. 27 Dec.	Richard & Ester *Martin*	Bricklayer
79.	1 Mar.	*Frances* b. 22 Jan.	Samuel & Mary *Sharp*	Labourer
82.	10 May	*Ellen Ellis* b. 15 Mar.	Illegitimate daughter of Charlotte *Swift*	Widow
83.	7 June	*Samuel* b. 6 May	Samuel & Eliz. *Greenyer*	Labourer
89.	8 Nov.	*Henry* b. 29 Sept.	James & Ann *Baker*	Shepherd
		1819		
93.	17 Jan.	*Jane* b. 17 Oct.	Illegitimate daughter of Elizabeth *Sharp*	Servant
94.	31 Jan.	*Caroline* b. 9 Jan.	William & Mary *Hollingdale*	Labourer
97.	11 April	*Mary* b. 6 Mar.	Thomas & Jane *Kimber*	Labourer
100.	9 May	*John* b. 21 Feb.	John & Charlotte *Taylor*	Carpenter
101.	17 June	*Jane* b. 14 June	John & Charlotte *Carver*	Yeoman
118.	9 April	*Robert* b. 2 Mar.	Richard & Ester *Martin*	Bricklayer
		1821		
139.	8 April	*Elizabeth*	Thomas & Jane *Kimber*	Labourer
144.	1 July	*James*	James & Anne *Grinyer*	Carter
145.	15 July	*Jane*	Henry & Jane *Gobel*	Labourer
147.	12 Aug.	*Ephraim* b. 7 Mar.	John & Mary *Sharp*	Blacksmith
148.	16 Sept.	*William*	Edward & Frances *Kimber*	Labourer
		1822		
167.	14 July	*James*	Richard & Ester *Martin*	Labourer
		1823		
179.	6 April	*Samuel*	Samuel & Latitia *Hampton*	Shoemaker
184.	22 June	*Jane*	Thomas & Jane *Kimber*	Labourer
194.	2 Nov.	*Suzan*	Edward & Frances *Kimber*	Labourer

Parish registers can also be used to work out when epidemics (mass illnesses) hit an area. For instance in 1832 and 1848 the numbers of burials registered in many parishes is much higher than normal especially in towns. There were cholera epidemics in these years.

By itself, a register of burials tells us a lot about when people died and how old they were, but it tells us little about anything else. It does not tell us what the people did for a living or even who was related to who. Look at E again. In 1819 the name Ann Pullen appears twice. Was one Ann the mother of the other? Were all the 'Kimbers' from the same family? The Register of Burials does not answer these questions.

By looking at the registers of baptisms and marriages we can begin to piece together the lives of individual people and families. F gives a few of the entries in the Lancing Register of Baptisms between 1814 and 1823. Use it to work out the following:

1 What kinds of jobs did most people in Lancing do?
2 Was Ann Pullen the mother of Ann?
3 Why do you think the name 'Frances Cussans' appears in the register in both 1814 and 1815?
4 What relation was Sarah Kimber (born 1815) to Mary Kimber (born 1819)?
5 Now draw up on a bit of rough paper what you can piece together of the Kimber family tree. Write next to their names when they died (where this is given in the Register of Burials). Do the same for the Martin family and one other family of your choice.

The Lancing Register of Burials does not show when all these people died. Many of them moved away, so their burials will have been registered in other parishes. In any case if we are to trace many of the women we need to know who they married. So we can find out more about the lives of some of these people by looking in the Lancing Register of Marriages. G and H show a few of the entries.

6 What can you add to your family trees?

We must remember that these parish registers do not show births and deaths. They show baptisms and burials. People who were not baptised into the Church of England are not shown. Even so, as we have seen, they tell us some important things about the lives of ordinary people. We need other sources to fill in some of the details.

Census Findings

In 1851 a *census* (government survey of the population) was carried out in Britain. J comes from the 1851

Census. It gives us more details about some of the people we have looked at in Lancing.

7 Use these census findings to add to what you have found out about the Kimbers, the Martins and the other families you have looked at.

8 What do these findings tell us about the size of families in the middle of the nineteenth century?

G Extracts from the Lancing Register of Marriages

Thomas Baker, ____ of _this_ Parish,
Bachelor,
Elizabeth Coleman, ____ of _this_ Parish,
Spinster.
re married in this _Church_ by _Banns_ ____ with Confent of
her mother ____ this _thirteenth_ Day of
October. in the Year One thoufand eight hundred and _thirteen_.
By me ____ _Wm Feilde. Vicar of Lancing_.
is Marriage was folemnized between us { _The mark + of Thomas Baker_
{ _The mark ⌐ of Elizabeth Coleman_
the Prefence of { _Elizabeth Coleman's mark_ }
{ _Richard Steel_.
o. 2.

____

Richard Martin, Bachelor, ____ of _this_ Parifh,
Esther Inkpen, Maiden, ____ of _this_ Parifh,
re married in this _Church_ by _Banns_, ____ with Confent of
Parents, ____ this _twentieth_ Day of
March, in the Year One thoufand eight hundred and _feventeen_.
By me ____ _Matthew Feilde, Vicar_.
this Marriage was folemnized between us { _Richard Martin_
{ _Esther Inkpen_,
the Prefence of { _Th.S Miller_
{ _E. Miller_
o. 14.

H Marriages in Lancing

1823 William Knight married Mary Kimber
Thomas Knight married Emily Kimber

1830 William Cussans married Mary Martin
David Butcher married Susan Kimber

1834 James Kimber married Sarah Burchalle

1836 William Grinyer married Charlotte Knight

1837 Henry Page married Frances Sharp

1842 Alfred Sharp married Harriet Plumer
Samuel Grinyer married Ellen Grinyer

1845 John Randel married Susan Kimber
John Bashford married Sarah Kimber
John Sharp married Elizabeth Clapshoe

1846 Robert Martin married Mary Prescott

1847 Stephen Grover married Harriet Nash
Thomas Kimber married Mary Heather

J Details from the 1851 Government Census

Name of Each Person Who Lived in the House on the Night of 30 March	Relation to Head of Family	Married Single etc.	Age	Trade
Thomas Kimber	Head	M	58	Farm labourer
Mary Kimber	Wife	M	57	
Louisa Kimber	Daughter	S	18	
John Bashford	Head	M	30	Gardener
Sarah Bashford	Wife	M	37	
John Bashford	Son	S	5	
Esther Bashford	Daughter	S	3	
Sarah Bashford	Daughter	S	9 mths	
George Kimber	Son-in-law	M	17	Farm labourer
Mary Kimber	Daughter	M	13	
Frederick Bashford	Son	S	8	
Edward Kimber	Head	M	52	Farm labourer
Frances Kimber	Wife	M	53	
William Kimber	Son	S	23	Farm labourer
Edward Kimber	Son	S	20	Farm Labourer
David Kimber	Son	S	16	Farm Labourer
Jane Kimber	Daughter	S	11	Scholar
Elizabeth Kimber	Daughter	S	8	Scholar
Susan Randel	Daughter	M	28	Sailor's wife
Samuel Sharp	Head	M	63	Farm labourer
Mary Sharp	Wife	M	60	
William Martin	Head	M	33	Bricklayer
Ann Martin	Wife	M	31	
Ellen Martin	Daughter	S	9	
Emily Martin	Daughter	S	7	
William Martin	Son	S	3	
Edwin Martin	Son	S	1	
Robert Martin	Head	M	31	Master bricklayer
Mary Martin	Wife	M	36	
James Martin	Brother	S	28	
Thomas Knight	Head	Widr	48	Farm labourer
Jane Knight	Daughter	S	20	Housekeeper
Emily Knight	Daughter	S	18	House servant
John Sharp	Head	M	63	Blacksmith
Mary Sharp	Wife	M	65	
Kif Bradlaw	Visitor	M	58	
Thomas Tidy	Servant	Widr	50	Smith
David Butcher	Head	Widr	55	Farm labourer
William Cussans	Head	M	62	Farm labourer
Mary Cussans	Wife	M	62	
Samuel Grinyer	Head	M	32	Farm labourer
Ellen Grinyer	Wife	M	34	
Ellen Grinyer	Daughter	S	11	
Alfred Grinyer	Son	S	8	
William Grinyer	Son	S	6	Scholar
Felix Grinyer	Son	S	4	Scholar
Elizabeth Grinyer	Daughter	S	1	
Infant	Daughter	S	2 wks	

We can use census findings to find out a great deal about any community. For instance the 1851 Census tells us that there were 802 people living in Lancing, including 112 farm workers and 67 servants – of whom 80 per cent were women. (Most of the other women seem to have been housewives.)

Are you confused? You should be. Parish registers and census findings are not easy sources to use, simply because of the huge numbers of facts they contain. Can you see a use for computers in the study of history?

13 Fiction

Most fiction is of little use to historians. Most novelists are not trying to describe the world exactly as it is. The same is true of most of the films you see at the cinema or on TV. However this is not true of all fiction. Some writers and film producers set out to record in detail real events and situations which they have witnessed for themselves. Such novels and films can be useful secondary sources, even though the people in the stories are fictional. When you use fictional stories (books or films) as historical sources, think about these points:

a Did the writer (or producer) witness the things that he/she is describing? If not, where did they get their information from?

b Is the writer (or producer) trying to be factual and describe things as they really were? Or is he/she exaggerating or adding things simply to make the story more interesting?

c What were the reasons for writing the novel or making the film? Was it: to entertain; to put over a message or point of view; to educate people; simply to make money?

The answers to these questions will help you to decide how reliable the piece of fiction is as a source of evidence.

These pages look at one of the most famous novels written in the last 100 years, *All Quiet On The Western Front* by E M Remarque.

Eric Remarque was 18 when he joined the German Army in 1914 at the start of the First World War. He fought in the trenches for over three years. During the war his mother died of cancer and all his friends were killed. He wrote *All Quiet On The Western Front* to describe what the war was like for the soldiers who had to fight it. He wrote at the beginning of the novel:

(This book is not) an adventure, for death is not an adventure for those who stand face to face with it. It will try simply to tell of a generation of men who, even though they may have escaped its shells, were destroyed by war. **(A)**

In **B** and **E**, Remarque tells what happens when Paul, a German soldier, comes home on leave. Paul has been looking forward to this leave for months. When he arrives home he finds his mother ill in bed:

Suddenly my mother seizes hold of my hand and asks: "Was it very bad out there Paul?" Mother (Paul thinks) what should I answer to that! You would not understand. And you shall never know. Was it bad, you ask – you, mother – I
shake my head and say: "No, mother, not so very bad, there are always a lot of us together so it isn't so bad."

"Yes, but Heinrich was here just lately and said it was terrible out there now, with the gas and all the rest of it." She is worrying about me. Should I tell her how we once found three enemy trenches with their soldiers all rigid, against the trench wall, in the dug-outs, just where they were, the men stood and lay about, with blue faces, dead?

"No mother, that's only talk," I answer, "there's not very much in what Heinrich says. You see for instance, I'm well and fit . . ." **(B)**

Photographs **C** and **D** show the sort of scenes Paul would have witnessed in the trenches. Next, he goes to see his father:

My father wants me to tell him about the fighting; he is so curious in a way that I find stupid and upsetting. There is nothing he likes more than just hearing about it. I realise he does not know that a man cannot talk of such things. So I simply tell him a few amusing things. But he wants to know whether I have ever had a hand-to-hand fight. I say "No," and get up and go out.

But that does not mend matters. After I have been scared a couple of times in the street by the screaming of tram cars, which sounds like the noise of a shell coming straight for you, somebody taps me on the shoulder. It is my German teacher, and he at once asks me the usual question: "Well, how are things out there? Terrible, terrible, eh? Yes it is dreadful, but we must carry on. And after all, you do at least get decent food out there, so I hear. You look well, Paul, and fit. Naturally it is worse here. Naturally. The best for our soldiers every time, that goes without saying."

He drags me along to a table with a lot of others. They welcome me, a headmaster shakes hands with me and says: "So you come from the front? What is the spirit like out there? Excellent, eh, excellent?" I explain that no one would be sorry to be back home. He laughs a good deal. "I can well believe it! But first you have to give the Froggies a good hiding . . ." They argue about which areas we ought to keep after the war. The headmaster wants to have at least the whole of Belgium, the coal-areas of France, and a slice of Russia. Then he begins to tell us just where in France the break-through must come, and turns to me: "Now shove a bit out there with your everlasting trench warfare. Smash through the enemy and then there will be peace."

I reply that in our view a break-through may not be possible. The enemy may have too many reserves. Besides the war may be rather different from what people think. He

C Dead German soldiers, after the Battle of Cambrai, November 1917

D German troops on the attack

dismisses the idea out of hand and informs me I know nothing about it. "The details, yes," says he, "but I am talking about the war as a whole. And of that you are not able to judge. You see only your little sector (area of the front) and so cannot make any general survey. You do your duty, you risk your lives, that deserves the highest honour – every man of you ought to have the Iron Cross – but first of all the enemy line must be broken through in Flanders and then swept from the field." He blows his nose and wipes his beard. "Completely swept from the field they must be. And then to Paris."

I would like to know just how he pictures it to himself, and pour down the third glass of beer. I break away. He stuffs a few more cigars into my pocket and sends me off with a friendly slap. "All the best! I hope we will soon hear something worth while from you."

I imagined leave would be different from this. Indeed, it was different a year ago. It is I of course that have changed. A year ago I knew nothing about the war, we had only been in the quiet sectors. But now I see that I have been crushed without knowing it. I find I do not belong here any more, it is a foreign world . . .

What is leave? A pause that only makes everything after it so much worse. Already we begin to think about my parting. My mother watches me silently – I know she counts the days – every morning she is sad. It is one day less. She has put away my pack, she does not want to be reminded by it . . .

I ought never to have come here. Out there I didn't care and didn't even hope – I will never be able to be so again.

I ought never to have come on leave. ❯ (E)

??????????????

1 Answer questions **a** to **c** at the beginning of this chapter. Do you think this story reliable as a source of evidence?

2 a Why does Paul tell people at home so little about life at the front (**B**)?
b What is there to suggest that the people at home are completely out of touch with life at the front?
c What does Paul think of the teacher and the headmaster described in **E**?

3 a In what ways does Paul seem to have been 'destroyed by war' (**A**)?
b What is there in **B** and **E** to suggest that Eric Remarque may well be writing about himself in *All Quiet on the Western Front.*

4 Remarque wrote the book about ten years after the First World War ended. Does this make it less or more reliable as a source of evidence? Why?

14 Roots: Reliving the Past

Do you ever day-dream in school, imagining you are somewhere else? Using your imagination is very important when learning about the past. As historians we must often try to put ourselves in the position of the people we are studying. This helps us to find out just what it must have been like to have lived through the events that they lived through. By 'putting ourselves in their shoes' we can begin to work out why they behaved as they did, and 're-live the past' in our minds. Alex Haley shows how this can be done in his book *Roots*.

Alex Haley, a black American, had always been fascinated by the stories his grandmother used to tell about his ancestors:

'*The furthest-back person they ever talked about was a man they called "the African" whom they always said had been brought to this country on a ship to some place that they called "Naplis"* (Annapolis in Maryland). *They said he was bought by a "Massa John Waller" who had a plantation in a place called "Spotsylvania County, Virginia". They would tell how the African kept trying to escape and how at the fourth attempt he was unlucky enough to be caught by two white slave-catchers, who cut off his foot as a punishment. This African's life had been saved by a Dr William Waller who bought the African for his own plantation. Though the African was now crippled he could do some work in the vegetable garden.*

Grandma and the others said that Africans fresh off slave ships were given names by their massas (masters). This African was called Toby. He always declared that his name was Kunta Kinte. Later he married a woman slave called Bell and they had a daughter called Kizzy. As she grew up the African used to tell Kizzy stories about himself, his people and his homeland. He even taught her African names for things — he used to call the river that ran through the plantation the "Kamby Bolongo". He told her how he had been kidnapped: he said that he had been out in the forest not far from his village, chopping wood to make a drum, when he had been surprised by four men and taken away as a slave.' (A)

Alex often asked his grandmother to tell him more about the African, but that was all she knew. In his history lessons at school Haley learned more about slavery and the slave trade.

He learned that nearly all black Americans and West Indians are descended from African slaves. The 'slave trade' had been started by English seamen in the 1580s and it went on for over 250 years. Many European and American traders made their fortunes in the 'trade triangle' (C). The original slaves were captured in West Africa and brought over to America in cargo ships. **D** shows how they were packed in. The ships took between six weeks and three months to make the 'middle passage' across the Atlantic. Once in America or the West Indies the slaves were sold by auction. Then they were forced to work in the tobacco, sugar or cotton plantations. Cartoon **E** was drawn in 1830. It shows how the slaves were often treated. Alex learned that slavery was not ended in the US until after the American Civil War (1861–65).

For 40 years Alex Haley was haunted by the story of his ancestor Kunta Kinte. When he retired he set out to find out more about this man and to write his story down. It took Alex 12 years.

Language experts worked out from the 'African' words Kizzy had learned from her father that he had come from Gambia in West Africa. (Kamby Bolongo means Gambia River.) Gambian historians managed to trace the very village that the Kinte family came from.

'*Then they told me of something which I'd never dreamed of: there are very old men called "griots" in the older back country villages who were living, walking records of oral (spoken) history. They can tell on special occasions the centuries old histories of villages, of tribes, of families and of great heroes. Throughout the whole of black Africa such histories have been*

C The triangular route of the slave traders

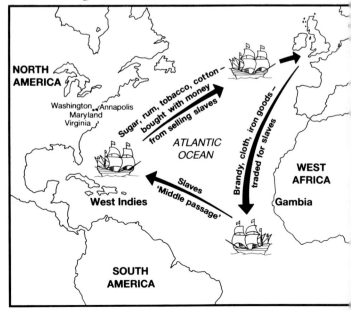

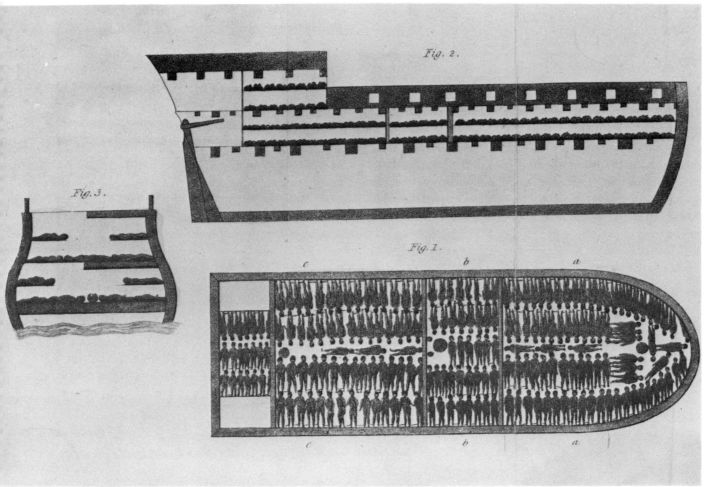

D Cross-section of a slave ship, showing how the captives were packed in

handed down by word of mouth since ancient times. I was told that there were some griots who could tell about African history for as long as three days without ever repeating themselves.

(Haley visited one of these griots, with an interpreter . . .)

He began to recite to me the history of the Kinte family as it had been passed down over the centuries. After two hours he said: "In the years between 1750 and 1760 Omoro Kinte had four sons whose names were Kunta, Lamin, Suwadu and Madi. About the time the King's soldiers came (1767) the eldest of these four sons, Kunta, went away from his village to chop wood and he was never seen again . . ."

In my mind's eye I began to imagine what I'd read of how millions of our ancestors had been enslaved. Many thousands were kidnapped away from their villages as my ancestor had been, but millions had come awake screaming in the night, dashing out to find their villages being raided and often in flames. The captured men and women being linked neck by neck with thongs and marched off in procession. I imagined the many dying or being left to die when they were too weak to go on towards the coast. And those who made it to the beach being branded with sizzling irons. I imagined them being lashed and dragged towards the boats, their screams and clawing with

their hands to get one last hold on the Africa which had been their home. I imagined them shoved, beaten, jerked down into the ships' stinking holds and chained onto the shelves, often packed so tightly that they had to lie on their sides like spoons in a drawer . . . **(F)**

After many more months Haley was able to trace the actual ship that Kunta Kinte must have sailed on. The *Lord Ligonier* had sailed from the Gambia River on 5 July 1767, reaching Annapolis on 29 September 1767. The ship had sailed with 140 slaves. 92 were still alive at the end of the voyage. Haley used all the evidence he could find to work out what conditions were like on the slave ships. He even went on a modern cargo ship across the Atlantic:

Each evening I climbed down the ladders into the dark, cold cargo hold. Stripping to my underwear I lay on my back on a rough bare plank and forced myself to stay there through all ten nights of the crossing, trying to imagine what did he see, hear, feel, smell, taste – and above all think . . . **(G)**

Haley now knew what life must have been like for Kunta Kinte on the 'middle passage':

'The stinging bites and then the itching of the lice grew worse and worse. In the filth, the lice as well as the fleas swarmed all over the hold (inside of the ship). His armpits felt as though they were on fire.

He kept having thoughts of springing up and running away. The worst thing was that he couldn't move anywhere. He felt he wanted to bite through his chains . . .

Kunta had lost track of time. The urine, vomit and sewage stank all around him. It had spread into a thick paste, covering the hard planking of the long shelves on which they lay. Just when he had begun to think that he couldn't stand it any more, eight men came down the hatchway cursing loudly. They carried long brushes and tubs. Kunta saw that they were not wearing any clothes.

These naked whitemen began vomiting at once. They went along the aisle scraping some of the mess into the tubs. But when they finished their job and were gone, there was no difference in the hot, awful, choking stench of the hold . . .'

Sometimes the slaves were taken up on deck to be washed down.

'. . . The first open daylight in nearly 15 days hit Kunta like a hammer between his eyes. He tried to cover his face with his hands. Fumbling blindly ahead on the deck he took a deep breath of sea air – the first of his life. The shock of the fresh air was so great that Kunta was sick at once. All about him he heard more vomiting, chains clanking, lashes meeting flesh, and shrieks of pain. When another whip ripped across his back, Kunta slit open his eyes to see which of the white men was whipping him . . . They were all soon being shoved and whipped towards where another chain of men were being doused (showered) with sea water. Then other white men were

E Many slave-owners were cruel men, who treated their slaves very harshly

scrubbing the screaming men. Kunta screamed too as the drenching salt water hit him, stinging like fire in his own bleeding whip cuts and the burned place on his back. He cried even louder as the stiff brush bristles not only scraped off some of his body's crusted filth but also tore open his scabbed lash cuts . . . '

Some of the slaves managed to kill themselves. Sometimes they did this by jumping over the side:

'. . . Suddenly, one of the girls was struggling wildly between the guards. As several of them went clutching and diving for her, she hurled herself screaming over the rail and went plunging downwards . . . then the white men up in the sails were yelling and pointing towards the water. Turning in that direction, the naked people saw the girl bobbing in the waves — and not far away, a pair of dark fins swimming swiftly towards her. Then came another scream — a blood-chilling one — then a frothing and thrashing, and she was dragged from sight, leaving only a redness in the water where she had been . . . '

As the voyage went on, many of the slaves died. Conditions in the hold got worse and worse:

'. . . The only thing that could take Kunta's mind off the white men, and how to kill them, was the rats, which had become bolder and bolder with each passing day. Their nose whiskers would tickle between Kunta's legs as they went to bite a sore that was bleeding or running with pus. But the lice preferred to bite him on the face, and they would suck at the liquids in the corners of Kunta's eyes . . . He would squirm his body, with his fingers darting and pinching to crush any lice that he managed to trap. But worse than even the lice and rats was the pain in Kunta's shoulders, elbows and hips, stinging now like fire from the weeks of steady rubbing against the hard rough boards beneath him. He had seen the raw patches on the other men when they were on deck, and his own cries joined theirs whenever the ship pitched or rolled more than usual.

And Kunta had seen that when they were up on deck some of the men had begun to act like zombies. Their faces showed that they were no longer afraid, because they no longer cared whether they lived or died. Even when the whips lashed them they would only react slowly. And some of them fell limply on their sides. They were unable to move. The white men would have to carry them back into the hold. Even before these men died, which most of them did, Kunta knew that in some way they had willed themselves to die. ' (H)

The slave ships stank so much that it was said they could often be smelt miles downwind. In the year that Kunta Kinte was taken to America, 100 000 other Africans were transported across the Atlantic as slaves. It has been estimated that in 250 years 20 million slaves crossed the Atlantic. 12 million survived the voyage.

Alex Haley has written:

'My own ancestors' story is really the story of all African—descent people (in America and the West Indies) who are all the seeds of some one like Kunta Kinte who was born and grew up in some black African village, some one who was captured and chained down in one of those slave ships that sailed the same ocean.

I hope that this story of our people can help to change the results of the fact that most histories have been written by the winners. ' (J)

??????????????

1 What point is cartoon **E** making?

2 a What did Alex Haley do to get a better idea of what it must have been like for slaves on the middle passage?

b Most of the details in **H** are probably true. Which parts, if any, might be untrue? Why do you think so?

c What sources might Haley have used to help him write **A**, **F** and **H**?

3 Imagine *you* are a black African who is kidnapped and taken to America or the West Indies as a slave in the eighteenth century. Write down some of the things that happen to you from the time of your capture to when you arrive on a plantation. Use the evidence in this chapter — but also think about how *you* would have felt. (To help your imagination, think about the last time you were homesick; the last time you were travel-sick; whether you mind other people ordering you around; whether you would have survived the middle passage or lost the will to live.)

Now swap your story with a friend.

How would a historian check that the story is telling the truth?

What questions might it suggest to him or her?

4 In Britain we have few details about the history of people who lived in the British Isles before the Romans came in 55 BC. This is because things were not written down. The griots of West Africa are able to recite the history of their tribes and villages over many centuries, *without* writing, for they know it off by heart. Do we need to change what we said about oral evidence at the beginning of this book?

5 What do you know about *your* ancestors, or those of the family you live in? See how far back you can trace the family tree. You may find you want to know more about some of your family's ancestors!

15 Case Study: The Mystery of the *Lusitania*

THE SINKING

On 7 May 1915, during the First World War, the Cunard passenger liner *Lusitania* was sunk by a German submarine *U-20* off the south coast of Ireland. 1198 people were killed, including 128 Americans. The sinking of the *Lusitania* was the first of a series of events which in the end brought the US into the war on Britain's side.

For the past 70 years historians have argued about what happened. The sinking of the *Lusitania* is one of the greatest mysteries of modern times. Some of the evidence in this case study may surprise and even shock you. You will have to make up your own mind about what really happened.

F An artist's impression of the sinking of *Lusitania*

In October 1915 the Cunard Shipping Company published its own 'history' of the *Lusitania*:

‘On 1 May 1915 the "Lusitania" left New York for Liverpool. Before the sailing threatening statements were published in American newspapers by the Germans saying that the liner would be sunk. On 7 May the Irish coast was sighted and at 2 pm the liner was within 10 miles of the Old Head of Kinsale. Without the slightest warning, a torpedo from a German submarine struck "Lusitania" between the third and fourth funnels. There was evidence that a second, and perhaps a third torpedo was fired, and the great ship sank within 20 minutes. Men, women and children vainly fought for their lives amongst the wreckage . . .’ (A)

In the days after the sinking the US consul in Ireland took sworn statements from American survivors. **B** comes from one of these statements:

‘Suddenly the ship shook from stem to stern and at once started to list (tilt) to starboard. Then a second and much greater explosion took place . . . The first lifeboat to be launched, for the most part full of women, fell 60 or 70 feet into the water and all of the occupants were drowned. This was because the crew could not work the lifeboat pulley systems properly . . . After about an hour we saw smoke coming towards us on the horizon, but as soon as the funnel was just in sight it went away from us again. This must have been one of the boats that the German submarine stopped from coming to our rescue . . .’ (B)

Walther Schwieger was the Captain of the German *U-20*. He watched the *Lusitania* sinking, through his periscope. He dictated what happened into the Captain's logbook:

‘An unusually heavy explosion takes place with a very strong cloud far beyond the front funnel. The explosion of the torpedo must have been followed by a second one (boiler or coal powder?) The decks above the point of impact and the bridge are torn apart. Fire breaks out and smoke covers the high bridge. The ship stops and lists over to starboard. Quickly the bow goes under water. Great confusion on board . . .’ (C)

Schwieger later told a friend in Germany:

‘The ship was sinking with unbelievable speed . . . Desperate

people ran helplessly up and down while men and women jumped into the water and tried to swim to empty overturned lifeboats. The scene was too horrible to watch and I gave orders to dive to 20 metres and away. **(D)**

The Cunard history goes on:

It was the foulest act of murder ever committed on the high seas . . . The "Lusitania" today lies at the bottom of the sea. Her name will be a lasting monument to the wicked crimes of a savage nation whose lust for blood knew no bounds. **(E)**

So the *Lusitania* sank within 20 minutes of being hit and most of the passengers drowned. There was an outcry in both Britain and America. Picture **F** appeared on the front of one British newspaper, *The Sphere*.

But the story does not end there . . .

COULD IT HAVE BEEN PREVENTED?

G shows how the sinking of the *Lusitania* was used to stir up hatred of the Germans. Could the disaster have been prevented? As we have seen, the Germans had publicly warned that the *Lusitania* might be sunk. In February 1915 the German Ambassador in Washington declared in a letter to US President Wilson:

The waters surrounding Great Britain and Ireland, including the whole English Channel, are to be a war zone. Every enemy merchant ship found in the war zone will be destroyed . . . Even neutral ships are in danger in the war zone because British ships often fly neutral flags. This means mistakes cannot always be avoided. **(H)**

G The memory of the *Lusitania* was used to encourage men to join up

??????????????

1 a How does Cunard's history (**A**) try to get the sympathy of the reader?
b What was different about the second explosion (**B**)?
c What do we learn about Captain Schwieger from **C** and **D**?
d What impression does Cunard give of U-boat captains and their crews in **E**?

3 F was drawn with the help of eyewitnesses. What message is the artist trying to put over?

4 How far can we trust these sources? Put them in order, with the most reliable at the top.

J Where the *Lusitania* went down

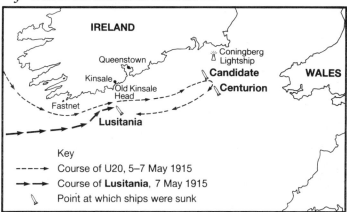

In the three months before the *Lusitania* disaster, German U-boats had sunk over 30 British ships. On 29 April the American ship *Gulflight* had been mistakenly fired on by a German U-boat, although not much damage was done.

At full speed *Lusitania* could outstrip any U-boat. On her last voyage she was not travelling at full speed. Cunard had ordered her captain not to use one of her four engines, because of the fuel shortage.

Map **J** shows *Lusitania's* route. Two days before the sinking, the Admiralty in London knew that *U-20* was still off the south coast of Ireland. Winston Churchill was First Lord of the Admiralty and the minister in charge of the Royal Navy. His deputy was Lord Fisher, a very old admiral (**K**).

On 5 May 1915 Churchill and Fisher had met to discuss the situation. The British warship *Juno* was patrolling the area. The *Lusitania* had been meant to join up with *Juno*, which would then have escorted the *Lusitania* home. However *Juno* was very old and not

K Winston Churchill (left) and Lord Fisher

properly protected against torpedoes. So Churchill and Fisher ordered *Juno* to sail into Queenstown harbour in case she was attacked. *No* signal was sent to *Lusitania* telling her captain, Captain Turner, of this. *No* new orders were sent to *Lusitania* to turn back or take a different route. Commander Kenworthy was at the meeting on 5 May. He later wrote:

❛ *The "Lusitania" was sent at greatly reduced speed into an area where a U-boat was known to be waiting and with her escorts withdrawn.* ❜ **(L)**

Kenworthy was never allowed to give all the details of what was decided at the meeting, because of the Official Secrets Act. After the meeting, Churchill left for France to see how the war in the trenches was going. He did not return to England until after the *Lusitania* had been sunk. Lord Fisher was left in charge.

Since then, historians have asked many questions:

● Did the *Lusitania's* Captain Turner do his job properly? Could *he* have prevented the disaster?

M Evidence *against* the Admiralty

1 Lord Fisher said in a speech at the Hague Peace Conference in 1899: *'Hit your enemy in the belly and kick him when he is down, and boil his prisoners in oil – if you take any – and torture his women and children. Then people will keep clear of you.'*

2 In September 1914 several newspapers reported a conversation that Winston Churchill had with the designer of *Lusitania*. The designer . . . *'told Churchill: "The Navy hasn't anything like her!" Churchill replied: "We have. To me she is just another 45 000 tons of livebait."'*

3 In 1914 all British ships were ordered to fly the flag of a neutral country when in British waters. A memo in Cunard's office stated: *'Pass the word around that the flag to use is the American.'*

4 On 23 December 1914 this signal was sent by the Admiralty to the British Fleet: *'In all action* (with U-boats) *white flags should be fired upon without delay.'*

5 Herbert Richmond, who worked at the Admiralty, wrote in his diary on 27 February 1915 that Churchill gave orders to the British fleet about U-boat crews: *'Survivors should be taken prisoner or shot – whichever is the most convenient.'*

6 Early in 1915 Lord Fisher said in a letter to Admiral Jellicoe: *'Winston completely dominates the Admiralty. His power of work is absolutely amazing!'*

7 Churchill and Fisher met on 5 May 1915. No new orders were sent to *Lusitania*.

8 On 6 May *U-20* sank *Candidate* at 7 am and *Centurion* at 1 pm. The attacks were reported to the Admiralty. No new orders were sent to *Lusitania*.

9 The US Ambassador in London wrote in a letter to his son on 2 May 1915: *'Peace? Lord knows when! If a British liner full of American passengers be blown up, what will Uncle Sam (USA) do? That's what's going to happen. We all have a feeling here that more and more frightful things are about to happen.'*

10 In 1914 Churchill had written in a letter to another minister: *'We need to get neutral ships caught up with the German submarines and the ships we most need to affect are the Americans.'*

11 Churchill wrote in his history of the First World War, *The World Crisis*: *'The plan which brings an ally into the field* (war) *is as important as that which wins a great battle. U-boats ran a great risk of mistaking neutral ships for British ships and of drowning neutral crews. Thus bringing Germany into conflict with other great powers.'*

12 Churchill believed the war must be won at all costs. His official biographer, Martin Gilbert, has written: *'There are many examples of Churchill's ruthlessness in trying to win the war. He was one of the first ministers to demand the bombing of enemy targets in towns. He continued in his belief that poison gas should be used against the Turks.'* (Turkey was an ally of Germany.)

● Was the Admiralty to blame? Did Churchill and Fisher neglect their duties?

● Did Churchill or Fisher *want* the *Lusitania* to be sunk, in the hope that it would somehow help Britain win the war against Germany?

N Evidence in the Admiralty's favour

1 In March 1915 Churchill had sent a large task force to attack Turkey (an ally of Germany) at Gallipoli. The aim was to knock Turkey out of the war and then move against the Germans from the east. It was a brilliant plan, and if it had worked Germany might have been quickly defeated. In April 1915 the plan had started to go badly wrong. By May 1915 the Gallipoli campaign was taking up nearly all of Churchill's time.

2 On the day the *Lusitania* was sunk, Churchill was in France. Fisher was left in charge of Admiralty affairs.

3 Escort ships could not have guaranteed *Lusitania's* safety. *Juno* had little protection against torpedoes. When Admiral Coke at Queenstown heard that the *Lusitania* had been attacked he sent *Juno* out to pick up survivors. However, when Lord Fisher heard of this he feared *Juno* might also be sunk. He ordered her back.

4 At 11 am on 7 May the Admiralty sent this signal to all British ships: *'Submarines active in southern part of Irish Channel. Last heard of 20 miles south of Coningberg Light Vessel. Make certain "Lusitania" gets this.'*

5 By the Spring of 1915 the war in France had reached a stalemate. Neither Germany nor the Allies were strong enough to break through. Thousands of men were dying every day. France and Britain badly needed the US in the war. If the US had entered the war in 1915 (instead of 1917) millions of lives – both allied and German – could have been saved.

6 Captain Turner could have taken avoiding action himself. He could have 'zig-zagged' the ship through the danger zone, making it difficult for the U-boat captain to aim. He could have sailed through the most dangerous part of the zone by night.

7 Captain Webb, who worked at the Admiralty, prepared a report for the Mersey Inquiry: *'The Captain knew he was travelling through a dangerous area in which submarines were active. Yet he travelled along the usual trade route at a speed about three-quarters of what he was able to get out of the ship. So he kept his valuable vessel for longer than was necessary in an area where she was most likely to be attacked, inviting disaster . . . We are forced to suggest that he is either completely incompetent* (without ability) *or that he had been got at by the Germans!'*

8 Winston Churchill was to become one of the greatest war leaders the world has ever known. In 1940 he became Britain's Prime Minister. Many historians believe that in the Second World War, Hitler and the Nazis would not have been beaten without Churchill's courage and leadership.

Tables **M** and **N** look at the evidence for and against the British Admiralty. Study them carefully. The questions at the end of this chapter will help you to make up your own mind whether Churchill or Fisher was to blame.

The sinking of the *Lusitania* turned the US strongly against Germany. But America did not enter the war until 6 April 1917. As the next section shows, there is another side to the mystery of the *Lusitania*.

Was the Admiralty to blame for the *Lusitania* disaster? Were Winston Churchill or Lord Fisher guilty of neglecting their duties or of wanting the *Lusitania* to be sunk?

To make sense of the evidence in this chapter we have to examine the evidence very carefully. Like detectives, we must remain on our guard:

● Is any of the evidence misleading or simply irrelevant (missing the point)?

● Are any of the witnesses trying to deceive us?

● What kind of people were Lord Fisher and Winston Churchill? Was either of them the kind of man who might have failed to carry out his duties properly? Was either of them ruthless (hard) enough to have allowed a large passenger liner to be sunk, simply in the hope that it might help in winning the war?

The questions on this page will help you to work out your own theories on what happened.

??????????????

1 Is there anything in **J**, **M** and **N** to show that Churchill and Fisher must have been aware that the *Lusitania* was in great danger?

2 a What do we learn about Lord Fisher from chart **M**?

b We know that from 5 May till several days after the sinking Fisher was in charge at the Admiralty. What evidence is there in **M7** and **M8** to suggest that he neglected his duties? What could be said in his defence?

c Is there any evidence that Churchill neglected *his* duties?

3 a What do we learn about Winston Churchill from chart **M**?

b What do you think Churchill meant by calling *Lusitania* 'livebait' (**M2**)? Is this a reliable source?

c What motive might Churchill have had for allowing *Lusitania* to be sunk?

d What evidence is there in **M** to support this theory?

e Look at **N**. What can be said in Churchill's defence?

4 Class activity Hold your own inquiry into the *Lusitania* disaster, with two members of the class pretending to be Winston Churchill and Lord Fisher. They should then choose two other members of the class to act as defence lawyers and advise them. The rest of the class should think of questions to put to Churchill and Fisher.

16 Case Study: The Secret of the *Lusitania*

Why *did* the Germans sink the *Lusitania*? Cunard's official history says:

The appalling crime was completely against international law . . . The enemy as expected then tried to justify his wicked work by claiming that the ship was armed. This was totally untrue. **(A)**

The German Government made a second claim. German Admiral Behncke said in a speech:

The explosion of the torpedo was followed at once by a further explosion of an extremely strong effect. The second explosion must be traced back to the exploding of large quantities of ammunition inside the ship. **(B)**

He said that the cargo of high explosives had meant that the passengers had been deliberately put at risk. If the German claims were true then under international law they had the right to sink the *Lusitania*. At the time, most people in Britain and the US were certain that the Germans were simply lying. American customs officials reported:

She was inspected before sailing. No guns were found, and the ship sailed without any armaments. **(C)**

In 1915 the British Government took sworn statements from all 289 survivors from the crew. 13 of the statements were given to Lord Mersey. (The other 276 have never been made public.) All 13 statements begin by saying:

At the time of sailing the ship was in good order. She was unarmed, possessing no weapons and she has never carried such equipment . . . **(D)**

These crew members said they believed that the *Lusitania* had been hit by a second torpedo. The government inquiry into the disaster reported:

Lusitania was struck on the starboard side somewhere between the third and fourth funnels . . . A second torpedo was fired immediately afterwards which struck the ship on the starboard side. **(E)**

However not all the evidence seems to fit. On 19 June 1913 the *New York Tribune* newspaper had reported:

Cunard officials admitted to a Tribune reporter that the ship is being equipped with high powered naval guns as part of England's new policy of arming passenger boats. **(F)**

On 16 March 1914 Winston Churchill said in a speech to the House of Commons:

Some 40 British merchant ships have been armed for their defence. **(G)**

The log of *U-20* reports that Captain Schwieger only fired *one* torpedo. He wrote in his diary:

I could have fired a second into those throngs of people on board trying to save themselves. **(H)**

U-boat captains did not have much faith in their torpedoes, and for good reasons. For instance on 6 May 1915 when *U-20* hit *Centurion* with two torpedoes, fired at point-blank range, the ship took over 1 hour 20 minutes to sink.

After the *Lusitania* was sunk the Royal Navy seems to have behaved strangely. A local fisherman, Edward White, tried to tow lifeboats containing about 80 survivors – many badly injured – into Kinsale Harbour. Walter D Fair described what happened in a letter to Alfred Booth, one of Cunard's owners:

They had arrived off the mouth of Kinsale Harbour and would have landed the passengers in another 20 minutes. Then they were overtaken by the Navy tug "Stormcock". Her captain, instead of allowing White to proceed at once to the nearest land, insisted upon the transfer of survivors to the "Stormcock". I understand that he threatened White that if he did not stop he would sink his boat. **(J)**

At 3 pm Lord Fisher had sent this signal to Admiral Coke in Queenstown:

Make sure that bodies selected for the inquest have not been mutilated (damaged) *by means that we do not wish to be made public.* **(K)**

Many old people at Kinsale say that after the Second World War a salvage ship *HMS Reclaim* moored over the wreck of the *Lusitania* several times. Some of the locals remember hearing explosions. The Royal Navy has always denied that *Reclaim* went to the site.

In 1972 an important US Government document was published. It was a sworn statement made by a man

N The sinking

called Dr Ritter. Ritter was an Austrian scientist who was in the pay of the British Secret Service in the US. He remembered a meeting with Captain Guy Gaunt, a British diplomat:

❝*On 26 April 1915 I visited Gaunt at his office. During the conversation we talked about explosives. He asked me what effect, if any, sea water coming into contact with gun cotton (a high explosive) would have. I asked him why he wanted to know this. He said: "We are required to send by one of our fastest steamers in the next day or so about 600 tons of gun cotton."*

I told him there were two kinds of gun cotton. One is not affected by sea water. The other is called pyroxyline. If sea water comes into contact with this gun cotton a chemical change takes place at once. This would cause a sudden explosion. He asked me what to do to prevent this and I said "Keep it in a dry place". ❞ (L)

Marine archaeology provides further clues. In 1982 a mini-submarine went down to the wreck of the *Lusitania*. The historian Colin Simpson tells us:

❝*Altogether we shot 28½ hours of video film and these have been studied over the last few months. They show that the Lusitania lies on her starboard side with much of her deck structure collapsed down onto the sea bed. They show that a determined attempt to salvage or at least work on the wreck has been made. There is also evidence that someone has been into the forward hold. There is a gaping hole in the bows, far forward of where the torpedo struck but exactly where the cargo was stored.*

Later we recovered an unexploded depth-charge, bearing the Admiralty's mark and dropped in 1946. ❞ (M)

The blast at the front of the ship appears to have come from the inside.

The documents showing what the *Lusitania* was carrying in her front cargo bay are in the Royal Navy Records Office in Bath. They have never been released.

N is one artist's impression of the sinking of the *Lusitania*. Pictures such as these were used to stir up people's anger against Germany. Yet on 29 March 1916, at a time when our ancestors were fighting and dying on the battlefields of Europe and on the high seas, Lord Fisher secretly wrote to the German Admiral Von Tirpitz:

❝*I don't blame you for the submarine business. I'd have done exactly the same myself.* ❞ (O)

We should not forget.

If you want to find out more about the Mystery of the *Lusitania*, read *Lusitania* by Colin Simpson (Penguin), from which most of the evidence in this case study has been taken.

??????????????

1 What claims did the Germans make about the *Lusitania* after she had been sunk?

2 Fill in your own copy of the chart below for each piece of evidence in this chapter:

Type of Evidence	What it Tells Us	Reasons for Trusting/ Not Trusting It
B Speech	The second explosion was much bigger than the first – caused by ammunition exploding.	**B** and **C** on page 40 also suggest the second explosion was bigger. But the Germans were not in a position to know what *Lusitania* was carrying . . .

3 a What reasons might the *Reclaim* or other Royal Naval ships have had for visiting *Lusitania*?
b What evidence is there in **M** that the Royal Navy had visited the wreck after the Second World War?
c Do *you* think *Lusitania* was carrying weapons or high explosive? Why? If the ship *was* carrying these things were the Germans right to sink the *Lusitania*?

4 What do we learn about Lord Fisher from **O**?

5 Draw a poster or cartoon of your own about the *Lusitania* disaster.

17 The Politics of History

In many countries in the world governments and politicians seek to control what young people learn in their History lessons. By stopping people learning the truth in history some governments try to control what they think. Pages 14–15 showed how the Russian leader Stalin had history textbooks re-written to show that he had played a big part in the Russian Revolution. The Nazis also stopped young people learning the truth about the past. A German woman remembers how her lessons changed:

❝ *Most of the old books were replaced by new ones. These had been written and censored by Nazi officials. Adolf Hitler's book Mein Kampf (My Struggle) became the textbook for our History lessons. We read and discussed it with our teacher chapter by chapter.* ❞ **(A)**

Mein Kampf blamed the Jews and the Communists for Germany's defeat in the First World War. So many German children came to hate Jews and Communists. These examples show how – by lying about the past, by making up history – politicians and rulers can increase support for themselves. It is not only dictators like Hitler and Stalin who try to use history in this way.

History is an important political issue in most countries. For instance 8–9 May 1985 was the fortieth anniversary of Victory Europe Day and the final defeat of Nazi Germany. The countries which did most to defeat the Nazis were Britain, USA and USSR. However no joint celebrations took place between these three war-time allies. *The Guardian* newspaper reported:

❝ *A war about the War is breaking out. Russian historians and journalists are trying to ram home the message that the USSR was far and away the senior ally in terms of military weight.*

(From 1941–45 75 per cent of the German army was fighting on the Russian Front.)
The argument is made more difficult for the West in that most serious historians of the war in non-communist countries now broadly agree with the Soviet view. Mrs Thatcher has ruled out international memorials involving all the main wartime allies including the Russians: "Each of us will wish to remember it in our own way and each of us in our own countries will decide what form the remembrance should take."

Britain and other western countries appear to have arrived at this decision in a hurry after signs that the Russians wanted to use their Moscow celebrations to tell the world about the USSR's senior role in the War. Dr Kohl (the West German

Chancellor) *pointed out that 65 per cent of the West German population today were too young to have witnessed Nazi rule.* ❞ **(B)**

June 1985 was the anniversary of another victory. Once again politicians argued about how recent history should be remembered. The journalist David McKie reported:

❝ *Despite the worries of some Government ministers the Archbishop of Canterbury, Dr Runcie* **(C)** *can be expected to be in charge of the service of remembrance of the Falklands Victory. Some ministers were not happy with Dr Runcie's handling of the service in 1982 in St Paul's to remember the Falklands Victory. He was thought to have been unwilling to sound too patriotic about the war.* ❞ **(D)**

Church of England leaders had wanted to use Spanish in part of the service as a sign of peace between Britain and Argentina. An historian pointed out:

❝ *I am surprised that the Prime Minister is so against the use*

C Dr Runcie, Archbishop of Canterbury, and Prime Minister Margaret Thatcher outside St Paul's Cathedral

of Spanish. The practice of praying for the dead of both sides is very ancient. Even so tough a warrior as William the Conqueror set up an abbey at Battle on the site of the Battle of Hastings just for this purpose. Even though he was sure that his cause was right he agreed with the Church that his soldiers should undergo religious penance (confessing their sins) for having killed fellow Christians in the battle. What is the point of a victory if you do not go on to make the peace secure by making your enemy into your friend? **(E)**

The Falklands War also raised questions about how history should be taught in schools. In 1983 the journalist Martin Walker reported:

The Falklands Campaign caused some real problems for the new history teachers who make a point of showing how events of the present day are affected by what has happened in the past. The magazine "Teaching History" looked at the way Argentine schools teach children an extreme love of their country. It compared this with the "crude and harsh headlines of the popular newspapers in Britain" (look back at *The Sun* cartoon on page 6). *"What hope is there for caring teachers when their classes are taught in newspapers about bashing the Argies? There are enough social problems in British society without the irresponsible press stirring up strong nationalist beliefs* (extreme beliefs in your country, above all else). *These go against the efforts of wise humanities teachers over the past 30 years to encourage understanding and interest in other cultures* (ways of life)."

These are ideas that tend to annoy Conservative historians and lead to campaigns in the popular press against "left-wing" teachers. It is an almost classic example of the way that the teaching of history can become a big issue in politics. **(F)**

The teaching of history in schools can even lead to disputes between countries. In August 1982 the reporter Barbara Casassus wrote:

There is an international row over Japan's censorship of secondary school history books. This screening of textbooks before they are approved for use in schools has been going on for a long time in Japan. Last year the Japanese Education Department rejected three books proposed for use in schools and greatly altered others, especially those on history and politics. Instructions were said to have been given for between 200 and 600 changes per book. These changes have upset the Chinese. **(G)**

Many of the changes concerned Japanese actions before and during the Second World War. In 1931 Japan invaded Manchuria in north-east China, killing many thousands of Chinese people. In 1937 they invaded the rest of China. (You can read more about the invasion in *Modern China* in this series.) Millions of Chinese people died, many being murdered in cold blood by Japanese soldiers. Barbara Casassus goes on:

Chinese newspapers have attacked the Japanese for distorting (making false) *history. They pointed out that the censors have replaced words like "invasion" with words like "advance" to describe Japanese actions in China. The censors are also said to have glossed over or removed accounts of mass killings by Japanese troops. This "re-writing" of history is seen by the Chinese as an attempt to justify* (make seem right) *the past attacks by the Japanese. China has made official complaints and is demanding correction of the textbook changes. A visit to China by Japan's Education Minister has been cancelled.* **(H)**

So history textbooks are often used to put over a political point of view. In the early years of this century most British history books strongly supported the British Empire. 100 years ago over one quarter of the land area of the world was part of the British Empire. Millions of people had emigrated from Britain and other European countries to settle in places such as Canada, New Zealand, Australia and Southern Africa. These white settlers took the land by force from the peoples who were already living there (Indians in Canada, Aborigines in Australia, Maoris in New Zealand and black Africans in Southern Africa). It might be thought that these white settlers had *stolen* the land. However history books such as *Our Island Story* (published before the First World War) said:

It was in April 1770 that Captain Cook first landed in Australia. At the time the island was inhabited only by wild, black savages . . .

In 1769 Captain Cook had landed in North Island New Zealand. He planted the British flag and claimed the land in the name of King George III. For many years no white people settled in New Zealand, for it was peopled by a wild and warlike race of savages called Maoris. These Maoris were cannibals, that is, people who eat human beings. After a battle those who were killed would be roasted and eaten by the victors. Yet although they were cannibals the Maoris were not nearly such a low kind of savage as the Australian Aborigines.

. . . In the days when Cromwell was ruling Britain a few men sailed out from Holland and landed in South Africa. There they made their home and they grew rich and prospered . . . Soon thousands of British people settled there.

(However the British and Dutch "Boers" kept fighting each other) *. . . In October 1899 war broke out. In the darkest hour one thing became certain. The little island (Britain) was not fighting alone. The Empire of Great Britain was no mere name. From all sides, from New Zealand, Australia, Canada, from every land over which the Union Jack floats came offers of help. Britain was not fighting for herself but for her colony, and in the struggle her colonies stood by her shoulder to shoulder . . . South Africa is now entirely a British colony and we hope that it will soon be as happy and as prosperous as any other British colony!* **(J)**

K An example of how Black and White have been *segregated* (kept apart) in South Africa

Our Island Story continues:

❝ *From the beginning of our story you have seen how Britons fought for freedom and how step by step they have won it. Until at last Britons live under fair laws and have themselves the power to make these laws.* ❞ (**M**)

The historian who wrote **J** and **M** is clearly putting over a political point of view about Britain and the British Empire. Although they come from a textbook **J** and **M** are about as one-sided as the most biased sources we have looked at in this book. Whenever we are given information about history, even by historians, we must stop and ask: *Where is the evidence?*

Our Island Story does not mention that most of the people living in South Africa were, and are, black Africans. Nor does it point out that the white settlers treated the blacks little better than slaves. Black people in South Africa are still second class citizens (**K**). Table **L** shows how whites in South Africa distort (make false) history taught in schools to help them keep control of the country.

L   How history is taught in South Africa

Since 1948 South Africa has had a system of *Apartheid.* Blacks are kept *apart* from whites and they are treated as second class citizens. Blacks are not allowed to vote. They go to different schools and colleges. They are not allowed to live in certain 'white' areas and they are not allowed to do some 'white' jobs.

J M Du Preez, a South African teacher has made a special study of history textbooks in South Africa. These textbooks set out to defend apartheid. They say:

1 White are better than blacks.
2 The *Afrikaners* (Dutch white settlers) have a special relationship with God.
3 The Afrikaners have a God-given task in Africa.
4 The Afrikaners are clever and strong.
5 The first white settlers were making their homes in a largely empty land.
6 The Afrikaners brought peace and civilisation to barbaric, warring tribes.
7 South Africa rightly belongs to the Afrikaners.

??????????????

1 a How did Hitler and Stalin increase support for themselves through changing the teaching of history in schools?
b What did the reporter who wrote **B** mean by 'a war about the War is breaking out'?
c Why do you think the British Prime Minister was against joint celebrations with the Russians (**B**)?

2 a How does the historian who wrote **E** use history to make a political point?
b According to **F**, what is the aim of history lessons in Argentina? How do newspapers sometimes encourage similar ideas in Britain?

3 a How did the Japanese government try to alter what Japanese children learnt in history lessons (**G**)?
b Do you think that the Chinese were right to be angry about it?

4 a What impression does **J** give us about the Maoris?
b Use your school library to find out as much as you can about the Maoris, then write down what you think they were really like. Say which parts of **J** are untrue.
c What views is the historian putting over about the British in **J** and **M**?
d Look at table **L**. What is the aim of history lessons in South Africa?

5 R Unstead, the writer of many school history textbooks, wrote in 1956:

'Our children are more likely to grow into the kind of race, that in our better moments we know ourselves to be, if they have been made aware of the qualities of men and women who have been admired from one generation to the next'.

Do you agree?